# THE GURUS OF INDIA

# The Gurus of India

SUJAN SINGH UBAN

FINE BOOKS (ORIENTAL) LONDON
STERLING PUBLISHERS NEW DELHI
EAST-WEST PUBLICATIONS FONDS B.V. THE HAGUE

Typesetting by Malvern Typesetting Services Ltd.
Printed in Great Britain by Billing  & Sons Ltd.
Guildford, London and Worcester

# CONTENTS

# FOREWORD

*The Gurus of India* is a timely book in a world that is beginning to recover slightly from the hectic intoxication of material progress. The path to enlightenment is a rough and difficult one and only a few rare individuals have ever made it to the end by themselves. Most of us need a skilled and experienced guide to show us the way—this is what the Gurus of the world are here for.

I can well understand and appreciate the sincerity and faith that is reflected in Major General Uban's work. It will, I am sure, gain him considerable 'karma' in the future. In addition, the author's personal and intimate knowledge of many true Gurus makes this book a very interesting one.

Most works on religious matters unfortunately tend to make very dull reading. I can give no better recommendation of Major General Uban's book than that it does not fall within this category.

THE DALAI LAMA

*30 November 1973*

# LIST OF ILLUSTRATIONS

# ERRATA

Read Bhagavad Gita throughout for various spellings

| | | | |
|---|---|---|---|
| p 23 | for Ðedanta | read | Vedanta |
| p 35 | ,, Hanivan | ,, | Hanuman |
| p 54 | ,, Kyderabad | ,, | Hyderabad |
| p 60 | ,, eigth | ,, | eighth |
| p 64 | ,, and | ,, | of |
| p 65 | ,, disciples | ,, | disciplines |
| p 68 | ,, praisworthy | ,, | praiseworthy |
| p 70 | ,, prople | ,, | people |
| p 72 | ,, Shabd | ,, | Shabad |
| p 72 | ,, sourch | ,, | source |
| p 90 | ,, are | ,, | care |
| p 91 | ,, indisposible | ,, | indispensable |
| p 93 | ,, intp | ,, | into |
| p 94 | ,, sint | ,, | saint |
| p 95 | ,, Sngh | ,, | Singh |
| p 96 | ,, sttempts | ,, | attempts |
| p 104 | ,, sme | ,, | some |
| p 112 | ,, iritual | ,, | spiritual |
| p 121 & 168 | ,, Kirshan | ,, | Krishna |
| p 121 | ,, staunchy | ,, | stanch |
| p 126 | ,, straighty | ,, | straight |
| p 160 | ,, Grasce | ,, | Grace |
| p 160 | ,, thuys | ,, | thus |
| p 161 | ,, preocc patiof | ,, | preoccupation of |
| p 164 | ,, nd | ,, | and |
| p 165 | ,, aone | ,, | at one |
| p 167 | ,, Perfece | ,, | Perfect |
| p 168 | ,, sicsussed | ,, | discussed |
| p 168 | ,, aso | ,, | also |
| p 171 | ,, Ayurtedic | ,, | Ayurvedic |
| p 172 | ,, kui | ,, | kin |
| p 173 | ,, ontemplation | ,, | contemplation |
| p 174 | The correct address for George Allen & Unwin is Museum Street, etc. | | |
| p 175 | for Rajdyoga | read | Rajayoga |
| p 175 | ,, Cassiver | ,, | Cassirer |
| p 175 | ,, L. de Jang-Keesing | ,, | E. de Jong-Keesing |
| p 175 | ,, Quandamayi Na | ,, | Anandamayi Ma |
| p 175 | ,, Swigh | ,, | Singh |

# ABOUT THE AUTHOR

Major-General Sujan Singh Uban, PVSM AVSM (Rtd), was born into a highly religious but liberal Sikh family in a predominantly Moslem area of the North-West Frontier of India, now forming part of Pakistan. His village house had a Moslem mosque in front and a Sikh temple in the rear. He imbibed all he could of the Sikh and Islamic faiths from his friends and he studied the Koran with reverence. He later attended the Gordon College, Rawalpindi—run by the American Presbyterian Church, where he learnt the Christian Bible.

Though a qualified physician and surgeon, General Uban volunteered for a combatant commission in the Indian Artillery so that he could make a worthwhile contribution during World War II, and later during the Indo-Pakistan wars of 1948, 1965 and 1971.

In the course of his Military Service he won two of the highest Indian awards for gallantry—the Param Vishishta Seva Medal and the Ati Vishisht Seva Medal—and throughout this period he never felt any hatred for the enemy.

At the time of Partition in 1947, Pakistan Radio paid him an unsolicited tribute on 10 September for his rescue, at great personal risk, of stranded Moslem refugee trains at Amritsar railway station, although he himself had suffered great harassment while coming out of Pakistan in charge of a train carrying Sikh troops and their families.

His contact with Hindu saints made him study the Bhagavad Gita, the Ramayana, the Mahabharata, the Upanishads and the Puranas. Later, he acquired some knowledge of the Buddhist philosophy from Tibetan Lamas who had taken refuge in India in the company of His Holiness the Dalai Lama.

His fascination in different religions and mystical practices led him to carry out a thorough comparative study, based on personal contact with some of their most outstanding adherents. All his spare time during military service was spent on these pursuits, the result of which is this book.

Since his retirement, General Sujan Singh has spent all his time, resources and energy on promoting the idea of universal brotherhood, peace and awareness of God as the solution of all ills afflicting the modern world.

The royalties of this book are dedicated towards this cause.

# THE QUEST

None holds ye but yourself
*Lord Buddha*

The urge to discover an awareness of the Inner Being has always fascinated mankind and has taken different shapes in different periods of human history. Physical satisfaction and material comforts appear to have been the aim of much of humanity, and some of the most destructive and horrifying wars were fought — and are still being fought — to gain material advantages for a whole community or a nation at the expense of weaker ones. When the ill-gotten riches of a whole empire and the surfeit of comforts resulting from industrial over-production could not satisfy that urge, man started thinking of the other ways of finding an awareness of themselves.

Every age has produced thinkers and philosophers who have made even more brilliant conquests in the world of the spirit than their materialist contemporaries in their field. Their thoughts, however, could not gain wide acceptance and popularity, due to a lack of sufficient 'spiritual culture' in a materialistically orientated society. But at all times there has been a limited number of men and women of faith and understanding who have benefitted from the lives of those truly great seers and prophets. Others merely contented themselves with the daily routine of being alive, however miserably and paying lip service to the dogmas of the religion of their fore-fathers and getting some solace from the writings of the departed Masters. For them the goal of inner awareness remained as distant as ever. One may get a veneer of faith which is so superficial that it cannot stand the test of even the slightest touch of adversity. Often one loses this faith permanently and then is adrift anchorless in the vast ocean of misery and fear called 'Life'.

1

It is good to be born in a church

but it is bad to die there.

*Vivekananda*

The times affect the mental outlook of the human race. Kaliyuga, according to Swami Shri Yukteshwar Giri, finished in 1700 A.D. and Dwapar Yuga is now running in its 276th year (1976). According to other thinkers, we are about to reach the peak of Kaliyuga. The idea is, therefore, one of destruction and soon after this would be the beginning of Satyuga. Whether we are entering Dwapar or Satyuga, there is, without doubt, a great awakening amongst a very large number of human beings, resulting not only in some astounding discoveries and achievements in the field of physical science, but also in a longing for awareness of God and spiritual advancement. Even the astronauts talk of God. The empty shell of religion is no longer attractive. The scientific mind is in quest of the Essence — the Creator, and the priesthood, which often wrongly presented God, has lost its hold on society. The Church is no longer held in such superstitious veneration. Even miracle men, posing as great Masters, and accumulating wealth, stand exposed, despite their big following.

Those seeking the Truth are on the march in quest of the One Mystery, the unraveling of which opens flood-gates of joy for those who persevere. The Masters are present in person to assist those who have started on the spiritual path in search of truth, for which, because of its complex and subtle course, they need an experienced guide. God's bounties are perpetual. Just as clean air, sunshine and water are necessary and available for the well-being of the body, so the supply of spiritual nectar is necessary and available for the soul, without which the body is of no consequence. It cannot be believed that God should have stopped sending spiritual Masters after a certain period. That God found it necessary to send Guru Nanak, Kabir, Jesus, Buddha, Mohammad, Zarathustra, Maulana Rumi, Shams-i-Tabriz, Abraham, Ramakrishna Paramhansa, Moses, Baba Sawan Singh and many others as

2

spiritual guides on earth, is a proof that human beings, because of their limitations, need a spiritual guide who can lead them on the way to God. How unfortunate it is that though these great spiritual Masters walk on this earth again and again, few can recognize them in their new body. Is it not tragic that we should be singing hymns in praise of our long departed 'Paramhansa' or Great Soul, whilst he stands barefooted at our door and even his knock at the door is not answered.

Behold, I stand at the door, and knock.
If any man hears my voice and opens the door,
I will come into him and will sup with him,
And he with me.

*The Holy Bible*

This book is a true reproduction of my experiences with some great saints of our times, most of whom, fortunately, are still alive. Through my experiences with them, I have become greatly aware of God and His importance to my life. Some have had a greater influence than others, but each has had an effect whilst preparing me for my next Master until, finally, I reached the end of my quest. These are the experiences of a common aspirant, who through God's grace, developed an intense thirst for this knowledge, fumbled and fell several times along this difficult but most interesting path and ultimately found himself at the feet of the one whom he himself considers the greatest master of our times.

This book is not meant for those who have already achieved their goal spiritually, or are well on their way, for highly evolved souls may not need a Guru. I have felt the need of a living master who could guide me along the path which my parents had chosen for me at the time of my birth. It is my belief that the recitation of sacred books one loves, purifies one's mind and prepares the soul for its upward flight. What brings about this elevation of the soul is the Nam, the 'Beej Mantra' or 'potencised mantra', which an accomplished saint alone is in a position to plant and later nurture with his infinite grace and love, in an aspirant's body. Since the body is the proper vehicle in which the spiritual goal is achieved, it has to be kept healthy and in good condition. Yoga exercises can therefore be extremely beneficial.

The saint, Master or guru one chooses has to be the perfect ideal of one's aspirations, a being one can always look up to. He should have perfect judgement and should radiate love and self-confidence. He should be a generous giver and not fettered by human bonds, a fearless exponent of the truth yet intensely human. True Masters are never exhibitionists. They encourage discipline in human society and they assist good government. They remain, at all times, engrossed in an awareness of God. On meeting your real spiritual Master, your heart will leap for joy, and your soul will cease its wanderings and start experiencing peace and joy in his company.

Our situation can be likened to a man who has walked into a vast marsh and even his most determined efforts only serve to make him sink deeper and deeper into the quagmire. The need then is for a powerful man on a firm patch of ground, to throw a strong rope towards him and ensure that it reaches the helpless man. All that the latter has then got to do is to hold fast to that rope which is his only hope, and surrender himself completely to the powerful pull of the rescuer. In this simile, which I have found most apt, the unfortunate man is the disciple in the quagmire of 'Samsara', the material world of illusion. The rescuer is the 'Guru' who is himself on the firm soil of Tapasya. The rope is the Nam, the Beej Mantra, which only an expert and powerful thrower can plant. Complete surrender by the aspirant is important for this operation. Any efforts to resist the pull of the rope may endanger the whole operation. Rescue is certain if the above conditions are fulfilled.

> Verily, verily, I say unto thee,
> Except a man be born again,
> He cannot see the kingdom of God.
> *The Holy Bible*

There is a definite design in accordance with which one is destined to meet the great Masters. In my case, it was an amazing series of events, nothing short of miracles, which brought me into contact with these great beings. Born and brought up in a remote corner of the North-West Frontier (now in Pakistan) and later serving most of the time as a soldier on active service, I had no reasonable chance of coming into contact with them. Yet, it is remarkable that a Bengali youth should become my friend in Peshawar, who was to introduce me to a great Master twenty-five years later and having done so, he was destined to disappear from this spiritual scene completely. As in many instances truth appears stranger than fiction, please bear in mind that although I have a natural liking for supernatural phenomena, I do possess a trained scientific mind and am not easily convinced.

My experiences are challenging modern science to focus its attention on 'internal revolution', because our external revolution appears to have taken us only towards callousness and destruction. In this period of spiritual re-awakening, there is an urgent need for individuals and societies to change their outlook if we are to live in peace and harmony. If more people would turn towards God, and so realize their true self, there would be no place for hatred and war. Love, the true elixir of life would play its part. There would be a revolution in our system of government and man would once again be man, assuming his rightful place in a fearless and contented society.

In India we have exponents of many different varieties of spiritual disciplines, and it is not difficult for a disciple to recognize the true Masters. There are Bhagatas advocating the chanting of Nam and the reading of scriptures. There are Yogis who teach Hatha Yoga, enjoining many physical disciplines, and some who teach transcendental meditation. There is the scientific Yoga path of Yogoda. There are masters who connect you with Nada or audible life stream, which once achieved, is sure to take you to eternal bliss and joy. No true master will ever ask you to bid farewell to your worldly responsibilities or practice tortures of the body in order to attain awareness of the soul which is the same as awareness of God. The greater the Master, the simpler his technique.

There are a great many Tantrics and some miracle men who have distinguished themselves by curing diseases, reading your mind and even fulfilling some of your worldly desires by the powers or Ridhi and Sidhi, acquired after certain strict disciplines with limited objectives. If your goal is of a higher nature, you will naturally shun these exhibitionists.

> The aspirant prays constantly to God to help him to contact a perfect Guru who will in turn take him to God.
>
> *Guru Granth Sahib*

Most of us die without using even a millionth part of our inherent powers.

> None is poor, O Bhikhu;
> Everyone hath got rubies in his bundle.
> But how to open the knot?
> He does not know
> And therefore is he a pauper.
>
> *Buddhist saying*

The need is to find someone who knows how to undo that knot and unravel the great mystery, which automatically throws open the flood-gates of perpetual joy.

> I have said ye are Gods
> And all of you are children of the most high.
>
> *Lord Jesus Christ*

My sacred quest took about twenty years of my life. Like a bee I have sucked from every flower within my reach to gather honey. God made it possible for me to see for myself the various paths through the eyes of some of their top followers. In His infinite mercy, God guided me to that prince of saints who quenched my thirst the moment I set eyes on him. Liberation of the soul appeared insignificant and of little consequence, and now my prayer is to thrive in the radiance of this master's eternal love.

> May the merciful God help you to find your guide as well!
> Body, mind and wealth; give all to the Guru;
> Obey his commands; thus is the goal achieved.
>
> *Guru Nanak*

My reason for writing this book is my earnest desire to help fellow aspirants avoid pitfalls while in their quest of God. Soldiering does not help one acquire any literary merit, you will notice many flaws in my composition and narration for which I offer my apologies. My only hope is that the aspirants will follow their own intuition in selecting their spiritual guide and not follow someone else whose very nature may be different from theirs. If this book becomes instrumental in

6

inducing some scientifically trained people to undertake this fascinating adventure into the spriptual worlds, I shall feel myself well rewarded. These scientists would then be able to sift truth from untruth and make it possible for much larger numbers to benefit from this experience in their own search for God. They must, however, appreciate that physical tests and intellectual equipment cannot perceive or assess something which is beyond their ken. A spiritual laboratory and spiritual instruments alone can help.

When I consider the benefits of spiritual orientation, I wonder why we are not putting our utmost efforts to a project which promises to be most rewarding for the whole human race. No budgeting is required. Every man and woman lives completely fitted with a laboratory and an inexhaustible store house which are never used. Infinite sources of energy and sustenance lie untapped which would suffice our universe to the ends of time, but we are unaware of them. May God put us on the right path.

SUJAN SINGH UBAN

# 1

## Shri Bawa Hari Das Ji Maharaj

On a Sunday morning in 1955, I was sitting with my family in Shillong. The weather was pleasant in this beautiful hill station, and the breeze blew softly through the pine trees, producing an uncanny effect on one's mind. Someone who had been introduced to me a few days earlier as an excellent amateur astrologer, and worked in the Audit Department of the Government of India, unexpectedly came in and we started a discussion about the best path for spiritual evolution. He talked about his Yogi guru in the Himalayas, who was reported to be 150 years old and his guru's guru who, according to him, was over 400 years old. He talked about some breath-taking miracles which he personally had witnessed, while staying in the cottage of his guru in those high hills. The narration was extremely thrilling and the man's character left me in no doubt that the account must be true. He mentioned how his guru fed scores of disembodied souls in his cottage on festive occasions, and of the appearance of dazzling lights when these souls arrived for the feast and the manner in which food for those who did not come, was despatched by mere thought process to their sanctuary in the Himalayas.

This kind of story is not uncommon in India. But when he told me how this guru had removed his disciple's soul from his body and made him face his soulles body, to realize the relationship between the soul and the body, I was amazed. I had never heard of anyone performing such an extraordinary act. Fortunately this Yogi Guru was still alive and could be contacted through another disciple, who was serving in the Forest Department. I had heard of and met a large number of yogis and sadhus but here was one without equal. I felt an intense desire to meet him and I carefully noted the address of his contact in the Forest Department. I was told by my astrologer friend that his Yogi Guru had no more than five disciples and did not appreciate any newcomers. He recommended that I should send a basket of fruits to the Yogi through this contact. If he accepted the fruits, I should go and meet him; if he did not, I should make no attempt, lest he got annoyed and cursed me.

Soon I found myself posted to the North at a Divisonal HQ, the jurisdiction of which included the Yogi's residential area. I took the first opportunity to visit units in the hills where this Yogi was. To my dismay, however, I discovered that I had lost his address and had even forgotten his name. But I had the address of the Forest Officer, so all was well, I thought. On enquiry, however, I found that the Forest Officer had died a year ago. I was heart broken. The only hope I had of meeting the yogi Bawa Hari Das had now been smashed. The orderly detailed by the unit to look after me found me morose and uncommunicative. He asked me why I was so miserable, whereupon I told him the whole story and ordered him to move out into the vicinity of the town and find out the whereabouts of a yogi who was known to be about 150 years old. He came back after a complete day's outing and gave me the happy news that he had found the address from an old disciple in the village nearby. He, however, could not guarantee whether the yogi would see me when we reached his cottage in the wooded hills, several miles away. I later discovered that this orderly was also one of the disciples and although he knew all about the yogi, he refused to divulge anything till he had consulted the senior disciple in the nearby village. How the only disciple in the army got detailed and planted as my orderly, to make it possible for me to meet Bawa Hari, was yet another miracle.

We walked together to meet him; myself, the orderly and the old disciple. The path was rough, uphill and full of tall grass amongst pine trees, where, I was told, cobras were quite common. The orderly told me, however, that cobras were harmless and were only there to protect this great yogi. There were panthers also, I presumed, for the same purpose. I had my own doubts about the capability of these wild animals to

9

sift good men from the bad; mistaken identity could spell a painful death.

Sweating and puffing hard, we arrived at the gate of the compound of the yogi's beautiful cottage. The compound appeared to be well wired-in and the gate, as usual, had been locked by the yogi, who, I was told, sat in his meditation room most of the time. With the door of his meditation room closed, shouts from the outer gate could hardly reach him. It was, therefore, all a matter of luck whether one could meet him. He came out to cook his only daily meal at about 10 a.m. and in a couple of hours he had cooked, fed and gone again. The only room inside had no sleeping berth and contained only a meditation seat. They said he never slept but had his rest during meditation. The older disciple told me he had first met Bawa Hari some forty years ago when he arrived in this jungle and started on his course of austerity. He was then about 100 years old, making him now about 140 years of age.

Whilst this man shouted to his Guruji to come out and open the gate, I was forming a mental picture of a very old man, bent down by age and hardly able to walk. Instead we saw a lean, erect and sprightly figure come quickly up to the gate, clad only in a white sheet from head to foot. He opened the gate and we all rushed to the gushing spring close by, to wash our feet and hands before bowing to him and touching his feet with our foreheads, a common salutation to yogis and sadhus in India. The yogi appeared rather curt when he asked me the purpose of my visit and who had mentioned his address to me. The orderly and the old disciple were trembling with fear, lest they be cursed for having brought me there, and so disturb his seclusion without his consent. I quickly told him the whole story of my auditor friend in Shillong and my subsequent efforts to contact him. He smiled when he learnt that my orderly had not disclosed the secret to me.

His stern face immediately became kind and charming. He said, 'My son, you must eat here today. I shall cook for you. A roast chicken with other special dishes await you in the Cantonment from where you have come. My food is going to be very simple and vegetarian, but it is wholesome and will do you good.' He was right. A magnificent lunch awaited me in the Cantonment where I was being honoured by a famous battalion. It would not be easy to explain away my absence from a party where I was the guest of honour. There was, however, no other course open to me but to accept the great yogi's invitation and stay with him a whole day.

The cottage was beautiful and had been the gift of his Forest Officer disciple, who had also brought spring water in a pipe line to his cottage, so making it really heavenly. Bawa Hari cooked his food in a steam cooker. It consisted of rice, some cereal and clarified butter with some salt. It was delicious. At his bidding on that day, twenty years ago, I became a vegetarian and a teetotaller. I had never been fond of drinking although during the British days it was a necessary social evil. But my vegetarianism was widely talked about in army circles, due to the fact that, since that day, eating meat has never really attracted me.

Hesitatingly, I broached the subject of this Yogi's Guru and the disembodied souls he sometimes invited to a feast. He said, 'The Guru is over 400 years old, and sits in that part of Himalayas,' pointing his finger towards a snow covered peak, 'and has to lift his overhanging eyebrows with his fingers from his eyes, so that he can see you physically.' He then explained how he had wandered for some twenty years along the coast of the Arabian Gulf and over the Tibetan plateau undergoing austerities and hoping to discover his Inner Being, all without any result. After he had become considerably emaciated and had lost all hope of finding his goal, he walked back into India, towards the lower ranges of the Himalayas and settled down in a decrepid old temple. He started singing 'God's Name' in that temple where some villagers would bring some milk or rice for him and join him in the devotional singing. One day a crazy fellow came from nowhere, whom no one in the village recognized. He had a shoe on one foot, the other being bare. As he entered the temple with one shoe on, the whole congregation shouted at him, pointing out the sacrilege he was committing by entering the temple with a shoe on. He just laughed and said, 'The whole world is God's temple. Which temple are you talking about? Anyway, I have come to talk to your miserable yogi priest', and taking this yogi by the

11

arm, he marched outside. As soon as they were out of sight of the villagers, he told the yogi, 'I have been sent by my guruji, who says you are now in a fit state to take initiation from him. Accompany me and I will take you there in a moment.' The yogi did not give any further details about his meeting and initiation by his Guru. He confirmed that this guru and many other sidhas, or evolved souls, sometimes visited him by invitation and were fed by him.

I asked of him if he could invite them on my behalf on Sunday, so that I could serve them the food and possibly have darshan. He said, 'You have not reached the stage when you can see them, but you will see the preparations and their disposal.' He said he was going to consult his guru. When he reappeared from his meditation room, his face was full of smiles. He said an American disembodied soul was present when he approached his guru and said that Sunday was a very holy day; a feast on that day would be welcome. The guru had, therefore, agreed to come along with seventy other souls including this American. On my return to the Cantonment, I discovered that that Sunday fell on 25 December—Christmas Day. The yogi, however, could have no idea of this without an English calendar. I was struck by the cosmopolitan nature of this spiritual fraternity and was all the more anxious to witness whatever I could of this supernatural phenomenon.

I arrived at the yogi's cottage on Saturday afternoon with the prescribed paraphernalia of food items purchased from the market. The old disciple also came, being a cook by vocation. We spent the afternoon peeling freshly plucked bean pods and washing everything several times over with the spring water. The whole night was spent in preparing food for seventy men. The menu was quite elaborate and contained some of the best known Indian sweet and spice dishes. The metal plates and glasses to be used for serving food were washed thoroughly by the three of us, the third person being the young son of the old disciple. The yogi took no part in helping us.

At 11 a.m. on Sunday, the food was ready, served in plates which were handed over one by one to Bawa Hari Das, who stood some eight metres away from us, at the entrance to the hall which was to accommodate the guests. He took about thirty filled plates with thirty glasses full of water. He said the remaining guests had not come and the food would be sent to them in their caves. He asked me to pray while the sidhas were eating the food, which I did. After about twenty minutes the empty and half empty plates and tumblers were brought out by the yogi and handed over to us. The first plate had been used by the yogi's guru and the prasad or food left on the plate blessed by the Guruji. Every plate and glass showed traces of having been touched, some only partially, while others were completely empty. The inside of the hall was not visible from where I was standing. No sound of any kind could be heard and the feast was over. My logical mind had some genuine misgivings and could not make out how such a vast quantity of food had been consumed without even a cough. The yogi would have been dead if he had eaten even one-third of that quantity. I toyed with the idea of having a good look inside the hall to see if the food had not been dumped into a deep hole there. I think the yogi guessed my thoughts since he went out of his cottage telling me that he would be back after a while. I went right into the hall and lifted the straw matting spread on the floor. I could discover no hole, no droppings, not even a few drops of water. It was a stunning experience.

Later during my long contact with Shri Bawa Hari Das, which still continues, I saw and heard quite a few unbelievable miracles which were rightly attributed to him. He is a remarkable man in every way. I have now known him for about twenty years and he looks the same, only a little leaner and more agile. His path of spiritual evolution is extremely difficult and may not suit a householder, but my respect and admiration for this man will never diminish. What I had read in the *Autobiography of a Yogi* by Yogananda, made sense only after I met Shri Bawa Hari Das.

I cannot forget a remark he made about the Yoga practices. He said, 'My path is extremely difficult. This time piece, pointing to an alarm clock, dictates all my activity. I have no powers to change it. My guruji is so strict that he nullified seven years of my austerities simply because I had slapped a self-confessed sinner in anger. I was put back in kindergarten.

13

It is much easier for a householder to be aware of God than for a yogi. His engagement in the battle of life gives him opportunities which are denied to a yogi. Had I known this before, I would never have joined this arduous path.'

A poor Brahmin had once brought his young daughter to Shri Bawa Hari Das and requested him to adopt the girl as his own daughter, since the Brahmin was in no position to get her married. The yogi accepted this and one day a Brahmin havildar clerk came to pay his respects to him. The Yogi felt that this man was a suitable match for his adopted daughter and therefore arranged the marriage which was quite successful. The havildar later became a subedar and both the husband and wife used to visit the Shri Bawa Hari Das often. Although the girl, when unmarried, was allowed to stay inside the cottage and cook for the yogi, after her marriage she was lodged in a room outside the cottage compound with her husband. The yogi had talked to me about the piety of this girl and the fact that even the yogi's guru raised no objection to her cooking or serving the food to them.

I had heard that one night after her marriage she had actually seen with her naked eyes the yogi's guru arriving by a flying palanquin in a blazing light. I was anxious to get the true version from her. By coincidence, she happened to visit Shri Bawa Hari's cottage when I was there. He introduced me to her, thus giving me an opportunity to ask her about the authenticity of her story. This is what she told me:

'I was just married and was staying with my husband in the outer room on one of our visits. My menstrual period had started, so I did not venture inside the cottage. One night at about midnight as I was looking out of the window, I noticed a flying palaki or palanquin, in a blaze of light. The cushioned and golden seats within the palaki were clearly visible. I saw some sidhas, looking very holy and impressive, sitting inside this object which was flying through the night without making any sound at all. I shouted for my husband to come and have a look at the guru's palaki. Meanwhile I started praying with my hands folded in the direction of the flying object. I noted that the palaki hovered in mid-air for a long time, for as long as I was praying. Then, with a blessing, it flew away. I pointed this

14

thing out to my husband but he only saw some burning light in the sky and could not see the palaki or the guru. Next morning Shri Bawa Hari Das spoke to me and said: child, you delayed the guru for forty-five minutes in the air by your long prayer. Only then did I feel certain that I had seen the guruji.'

This girl was very simple and I therefore took her story to be genuine.

Shri Bawa Hari Das had told me about his guru having dropped some good Chinese rice on top of his cottage when he had run short of rice, but he had never mentioned that his guru always came in a flying object. My auditor friend had also mentioned some dazzling lights on top of the yogi's cottage on some nights, but had not seen this palaki.

The world of the Yogi is a strange one, exciting in its possibilities and making the spiritual path attractive to many. Distinguished yogis like Shri Bawa Hari Das Ji Maharaj serve as beacon lights to those who wish to practise Hatha Yoga. Their powerful thought vibrations help humanity in more ways than one.

# 2

# Swami Yogananda

*The body is the horse on which
you ride on your way to God*
*Guru Granth Sahib*

The yoga system known as Yogoda which Lahiri Moshai
evolved and taught to his great disciples, Shri Yukteshwar
Maharaj and Swami Yogananda, is logical and simple.
Considerable literature is available at the Ranchi
headquarters of the Yoga Society, but I could contact no
outstanding Master who had perfected the art of this form of
yoga and who could teach it with any authority. After Swami
Yogananda, who visited and influenced the United States of
America considerably, the chairmanship of the Math passed
to an American lady disciple of Yogananda, the well known
Daya Mata.

I had the good fortune to meet this distinguished lady once
in Delhi, in the house of an army brigadier who practised
yogoda, and later at Dakshaneshwar in Calcutta. She wears
ochre robes and sings beautiful devotional music in English in
praise of God.

The followers of the Yogoda system as a means of becoming
aware of the Soul trace it back to Shri Babaji. He is said to be
immortal, remaining young from century to century and
assisting the great Masters in carrying out their spiritual tasks
in this world. How he initiated Shri Lahiri Moshai in the
Himalayas, close to Ranikhet, is an astounding miracle. It is
impossible fully to comprehend the true nature of Shri Babaji
due to his being a Maha-avatar, but his disciple Shri Lahiri
Mahasaya succeeded in carrying his torch with such brilliance
that he amazed all who saw him. Men of all faiths came to him
for help and they never went back disappointed. How he cured

16

the illness of an Englishman's wife who was in England when he was serving under him in India, shows the remarkable powers he possessed.

He asked his disciples to avoid theoretical discussion of the Scriptures. 'Solve all your problems through meditation.'

Seek truth in meditation, not in moldy books
Look in the sky to find the moon, not in the pond.
*Persian proverb*

Kriya Yoga, the technique of spiritual advancement taught by Shri Babaji to Shri Lahiri Mahasaya, who passed it on to Shri Yukteswar, who then gave it to Shri Yogananda, is a highly sophisticated yoga technique, consisting of breathing exercises and concentration on the psychic centres.

In his book *The Autobiography of a Yogi*, Parahamsa Yogananda describes Kriya Yoga as 'a simple, psycho-physiological method, whereby the blood of the human being is being discharged of carbonic acid and oxygen is added. The atoms of this additional volume of oxygen are transformed in the lifestream of the human being to regenerate the centres in the brain and the spine. By counteracting the accumulation of veinous blood, the yogi can reduce or even prevent the decay of the tissues. In this way mastery of life is obtained.'

I took a correspondence course and tried out some exercises, and since I could not find an expert instructor, I gave up this system for fear of damaging the nervous system of the body. It is absolutely vital that yoga exercises are conducted under the expert supervision of a Master. Having taken to physical yoga exercises, one tends to neglect the most vital aspect, the cleansing and elevating complement of chanting the Lord's Name, listening to devotional music or reciting the Scriptures. Great Masters like Babaji, Lahiri Mahasaya, Yukteswarji and Yogananda lay great store by it.

I have visited the Ranchi Centre of Yogoda where I saw a couple of young Americans who were seriously studying this practice. However, I saw no arrangements for devotional music or reciting of Scriptures. Perhaps that was left to the disciples to arrange individually, or the system had become so ultra-modern that the need for cultivating love of God, awareness of whom is the main aim of this discipline, was no

17

longer felt, the whole concentration being on the physical aspect. Daya Mata, however, enchanted the audience by her devotional songs in English when she came to Delhi.

Baba Sita Ram Das Onkarnath, who was to be my Master, knew all about this system and its great gurus. He reads the life of Shri Lahiri Mahasaya chapter by chapter every evening, along with other scriptures. Daya Mata met him whilst he was in silence or 'Mauna', at Puri, and at her request he allowed her to sit for meditation with him for an hour. She was kind enough to describe this experience to me when I met her at Dakshaneshwar. She had asked Baba after this meditation, why her spiritual progress had stopped and Baba readily told her it was because she was eating eggs. She was amazed at Baba's insight and confessed that although she did not take meat, she had found it hard, due to her American background, to leave eggs also. She summed up Baba when she said, 'He is God's own child.'

One of her young American disciples, who was looking for the samadhi or burial place of Lahiri Moshai, which was reported to be by the river Ganges at Hardwar, accidentally met me at Hardwar and asked me the name of the saint before whom I had just then prostrated myself in salutation. When I said it was Baba Sri Sita Ram Das Onkarnath, he rushed to prostrate himself at Baba's feet and said he had been instructed by Daya Mata not to miss meeting him whilst in India. For this purpose he had been to Puri in Orissa where Baba had last been reported and had been disappointed not to find him there. He expressed his delight to Baba Onkarnath in being able to meet him at Hardwar, while he was looking for the samadhi of the great Guru Shri Lahiri Moshai, about which no one appeared to know. The saint led this young man ten yards away from where we were all standing, and showed him the platform which housed the samadhi he was looking for. The amazing thing was that nobody, not even the caretaker of this ashram, knew about the existence of this samadhi. We were all stunned by the insight of Baba Onkarnath and the American young man was almost in tears with joy. How wonderful, he said, that he should achieve both of his aims of coming to India at the same time, that of visiting the samadhi of Shri Lahiri Moshai, and meeting Baba Onkarnath. The young man asked for a favour from Baba which was readily granted, that he should be able to meet Baba again next year.

Of all Yoga systems, Yogoda appears to me to be the best, provided one can find a real Master as a guide. I have known one man who had some ill effects while practising this by means of a correspondence course. It would be a great pity if we lost the technique of Kriya Yoga through neglect, though I know that the ever vigilant Shri Baba Onkarnath would choose suitable persons to propagate this system. Anyone wishing to practise Yoga should read the *Autobiography of a Yogi,* by Yogananda. This book, which makes one's hair stand on end, had a considerable and beneficial effect on my mind and induced me to study Yogoda. Unable to find a Master of this technique, I had to give it up. It appeared, however, to lay little stress on the essential ingredient of Love of God, which has to be specifically cultivated, before undertaking any Yoga practice. Otherwise the whole system is apt to degenerate into a desire for miracles.

# 3

## Swami Sivananda

The conjunction of the individual soul
and the Supreme Soul is called yoga.
*Swami Sivananda*

I had heard a great deal about this famous yogi and founder of
the Divine Life Society, and who had set up his ashram at
Rishikesh in the foothills of the Himalayas. I took some leave
from the army and went to stay with him, and was pleased to
find all the activities of the ashram which is located on the
banks of the Ganges, were well and neatly organized. From the
outer platform, one gets a magnificent view of the river, as it
starts its way into the plains after its Himalayan journey.
Rishikesh as a place of pilgrimage is the holy of holies, and the
spiritual vibrations of thousands of devotees constantly
bathing and praying cannot but have some effect on anyone
fortunate enough to be there.

I was given a clean room and a wooden bunk to sleep on,
both of which had been liberally sprinkled with disinfectant,
showing the interest Sivananda, a qualified and practising
physician, takes in hygiene. There were a number of European
men and women disciples in the ashram. Activities in the
beautiful temple above the road started early in the morning,
and continued throughout the day and some of the night.
There was a hall where yoga exercises, as prescribed for each,
were practiced by disciples and devotional chanting was
frequently heard. An Ayurvedic pharmacy and an eye clinic
for post-operative eye patients, were available for all in need of
such assistance. Swami Sivananda himself supervised
everything very carefully. The food was wholesome and free,
though you left your contribution voluntarily with the
Secretary at the end of your stay.

When I visited the ashram there was a large cosmopolitan congregation inside the hall where Swamiji was sitting on a wooden bedstead. Everyone else, including several European men and women, were squatting on the floor, though there was a vacant cushioned chair close to the Swami. I went in and touched the feet of Swami Sivananda with my forehead and was just trying to squat down with the others when Sivananda asked me to occupy the vacant chair. I pleaded that I could not occupy the chair in his presence and said that I preferred to squat at his feet. But he, in his magnanimity, insisted on my taking the chair, which in the end, I did. Sweets were distributed amongst the gathering, which then dispersed. The interview with the Swami which I had asked for was granted and I found myself alone with him except for his Secretary who stayed.

I explained the purpose of my visit and told him that yoga had attracted me from my childhood. He said that Hatha Yoga is not the appropriate answer for spiritual evolvement in Kaliyuga, because it is just not possible for everyone to undergo successfully the disciplines prescribed. He advocated Raj Yoga, a mixture of bhakti and simple pranayam or breathing exercises. He also laid stress on devotional music and the chanting of nam. He told me 'Yoga is not your line. You will get absorbed in bhakti. You will meet Guru Nanak, face to face, and will talk to him. Then you will realize that what I am saying is true.' He explained a simple breathing exercise which he said would help to keep the body clean and healthy. Meeting this great saint was heart-warming, as he was so full of cheer and limitless love for all who came in contact with him.

Having enjoyed Swami Sivananda's inspiring company for four days, I left for home. The hauntingly sweet memories of him always attracted me to Rishikesh whenever I was in that area. The last time I saw him, he was lying ill with pain in his back. Devotional singing was going on, and men and women were prostrating themselves before him and, as usual, leaving full of the joy of having met a great saint.

Then one day I was stunned to hear of his death. My informant was one of his philosopher disciples, who told me the news as if it were an insignificant event. I was angry with him for treating this great tragedy so lightly; one which brought tears to my eyes when I thought that I would never see his smiling face again. Mother Ganges had lost a great son, and Rishikesh, its main attraction. His spirit, however, still pervades his beautiful ashram. He prepared and left behind great souls who are in a position to show the light to a great number of disciples. Swami Chidananda adorns the chair now and when I saw him show great reverence to Baba Sita Nam Das Onkarnath, it was clear Swami Sivananda had left in him an eminent guru to help suffering mankind.

Swami Sivananda laid great stress on the singing of Ram Nam. He used to tell how Lord Siva had said to Parvati: 'Beloved one, I delight in Rama by uttering the Nama Rama Rama Rama. The name of Ram is equal to one thousand names of Vishnu.' Swami Sivananda said, 'A mighty power is latent in the singing of Ram Nama.' 'Scientists have now discovered that sound vibrations can have such tremendous force, that with them, silk can be cleaned more thoroughly than by a laundryman. But they have yet to realize that vibrations produced by the singing of the name of God will cleanse their hearts, will purify their souls and will remove all the invisible dross accumulated in themselves through many births.' He called this singing 'Sankirtan Yoga' or 'union by singing the Lord's name.'

He used to say Narrada had gone to Lord Brahma and said, 'Oh Lord, the people of Kaliyuga will not be able to practice austerities, nor perform yajnas, or pursue the path of Vedanta. Kindly have mercy on them and tell me some easy way by which they can attain God.' And Lord Brahama in his compassion, had given Narrada the Maha Mantra. By repeating this, people of Kaliyuga could attain an awareness of their Inner Being. This Maha Mantra is:

Hare Krishna Hare Krishna Krishna Krishna Hare Hare
Hare Rama Hare Rama Rama Rama Hare Hare

This shows the importance Swami Sivananda attached to the Love of God, although he was also one of the greatest exponents of physical Yoga.

He said: 'People cannot practice Hatha Yoga nowadays since they cannot maintain life-long brahmacharya or abstinence. Similarly, neither Raj Yoga nor Jnana Yoga nor Vedantic sadhana lie within their reach. Sankirtan Yoga is the easiest, surest, quickest, safest and the best way of attaining an awareness and love of God.

In Kaliyug Nam Sankirtan is the only support.
*Guru Nanak*

Baba Sita Ram Das Onkarnath says the same thing and lays great stress on singing of the Maha Mantra at all times of the day and night.

## SWAMI SIVANANDA'S EMINENT SUCCESSOR

I had the good fortune to meet Swami Chidananda under the most auspicious circumstances. The Divine Life Society, under his presidentship, held their annual All India Yoga Dedanta Conference at Delhi on the 29th and the 30th of December 1973. They invited Baba Sita Ram Das Onkarnath to inaugurate the function, in the Convention Hall of the Ashoka Hotel. They also asked him to agree to lead their procession, mounted on a silver chariot, through the streets of Delhi. With some persuasion, Baba agreed to join the procession immediately behind the vehicle carrying the deity, though he made them agree to his leaving the procession after about an hour, so that he could attend to his midday prayers. The silver chariot with Baba Sita Ram Das Onkarnath and Swami Chidananda sitting together, was an impressive sight. It showed the veneration in which Baba is held by Swami Chidanandaji and his Divine Life Society. Later, when Baba made an appearance in the Convention Hall, sitting beside the Swami, he uttered the word 'AUM' with such depth and resonance that the whole atmosphere was electrified. Baba declined to make a speech and asked one of his disciples to say a few words about his method of achieving awareness by 'ahar shudhi', pure satwik vegetarian diet, and by Nam Sumiran or the constant remembrance of God, which was accepted by the Swami as the essence of all Vedic philosophy and on which he later laid great emphasis.

An excellent souvenir booklet entitled 'Life Spiritual' was published on that occasion by the Divine Life Society for free distribution. It contains the photograph of Shri Baba Sita Ram Das Onkarnath, with the following note by Swami Chidananda:

## SHRI SITA RAM DAS ONKARNATH

After long periods of undergoing tapasya, the Lord Jagannath appeared to Baba Sita Ram Das and asked him to give Nam to all people. He has lived in akhand nam for over forty years and has proved by his divine life that by constantly repeating nam, and thus almost living in a state of nam, all other thoughts disappear. Then a stage comes when even nam stops, and then comes the great void which every yogi strives to reach. The soul takes the great leap forward from the state of relativity or dwait, to the state of the absolute or adwait. Baba Sita Ram is now in this state where everything external has fallen away from him, and is entering into the state when he sees Vasudevang Sarvangmiti.

This is a fine example of the spiritual insight of the Swami, since only a scientist can truly assess another scientist.

I have had yet another rare opportunity of enjoying the enlightening company of Swami Chidanandaji Maharaj. A delegation of 'World Fellowship of Religions' under the Chairmanship of Muni Sushil Kumaraji, the founding President of this organization, undertook a world tour in June 1975 to promote love and peace among all people. I accompanied this delegation, being the Secretary General of the organization. Muniji was also able to persuade Swami Chidananda to accompany us as co-Chairman.

Swami Chidananda's presence lent great charm to our proceedings everywhere. His innumerable devotees flocked the airports to greet us and filled the halls to listen to his eloquent exposition of the theme of God Orientation and Love and Peace for all.

However inconspicuous he tried to keep his presence, his devotees and admirers left no doubt in anyone's mind about the esteem in which he was held. This saffron robed smiling Swami carrying small cloth and paper bags, filled with odds and ends needed for the journey, would attract immediate attention and soon there would be a rush of people, all trying to touch his feet. His humility is such that on occasions he even manages to embarrass his admirers. When they are attempting to touch his feet he would touch their feet a little ahead of them. He has often played this trick on me and has endeared himself to me. Through his kindness, we stayed in Sivananda Yoga Vedanta Centres at several places in America. He took special pains to ensure that everyone was well looked after. One morning I found Swami Chidanandaji bringing me tea in my bedroom, saying that someone had delayed bringing it in time, so he thought it was his duty as a host to bring it himself. I have known no greater kindness or nobility. The Mantle of Swami Sivananda has rightly fallen on the shoulders of Swami Chidananda.

# 4

# *Miracles*

Someone informed me when I was stationed at Mhow, that a miracle man had appeared in a village outside Indore who could answer one's unspoken questions, cure incurable diseases and perform unbelievable miracles. Miracles would only happen on a night when there was a full moon, when a goddess performed miracles through the medium of this individual. It was not difficult to locate this miracle man since thousands visited him on days when there was due to be a full moon. On reaching the spot I met his daughter, one of the seven children of this simple villager, and established his background at first hand. He was a poor man who owned a small piece of land close to the village.

One day after ploughing his field, he returned home, dancing, whereupon the villagers thought he had gone mad. He was considered to be a simpleton, but his graceful dancing amazed people and they gathered around him. He told them, 'I am the goddess, so and so, ask any favours from me.' The villagers asked him to produce sweets to demonstrate his powers. He took some ashes from a nearby hearth, flung them up into the air and down came delicious sweets. In awe, all villagers bowed before him. Then he cured those with diseases by prescribing nothing more than the ashes of firewood. The news spread far and wide and something like a huge market sprang up in this unfrequented spot to cater for thousands of pilgrims on the day before a full moon. On other days the miracle man continued to undergo the drudgery of rearing a large family. But now, of course, there is no dearth of money.

After interviewing his daughter, I took my place in the queue and while I waited, I composed three tests in my mind. Firstly, I wanted to see some miracles with my own eyes to assess their authenticity. Secondly, I wanted him to produce for me a photograph of Guru Nanak and, thirdly, I wanted to know when, if at all, I would be blessed with seeing God or darshan.

I clearly saw the miracles performed for the three men ahead of me in the queue. For one he produced a miniature picture of Lord Krishna from a flower he plucked from the garland around his neck. For the second, he threw rice in the air and it came down as sweets. To the third man he offered his hand dipped in water and said 'You will smell whatever fragrance you name.' He asked for rose, and got it. Offering the same hand to the next man who wanted jasmine fragrance, he said 'It is jasmine', and sure enough it was. Turning to this same man, he said: 'You have come to ask me when your courtcases will end, and my answer is: only when you stop drinking. You drink and quarrel with your brother. Unless you stop that, the courtcases against you cannot end.' The man was in tears. It was absolutely true, he said, loud enough for everyone to hear. Now it was my turn.

He was a dark-complexioned man, rather effeminately dressed. He looked at me and said, 'As you have seen, I have already answered your question about miracles.' This was true. 'Here is the answer to your second question,' he said, and, plucking a flower from the garland around his neck, he produced from it a miniature framed picture the size of a thumb and handed it over to me. I noticed it was the picture of the famous Sain Baba of Shirdi, that remarkable saint of Maharashtra in whom Hindus and Moslems believe with equal fervour. This was not the picture I had wanted but before I could open my mouth to say so, he said, 'There is no difference between Sain Baba and Guru Nanak. Next time, I will give you one of Guru Nanak.' He had not produced the picture but had guessed my question correctly. From a secular point of view, Sain Baba and Guru Nanak are very similar, which, to some extent, accounts for their immense popularity amongst both Hindus and Moslem.

My third question seemed to baffle him and he never gave me an answer, presumably because the spirits who perform these miracles through a medium, cannot ascend higher than their own status. The wife of an officer, who had accompanied

27

me, had the disease from which she suffered, diagnosed correctly, but the medicine he gave had no effect on her. Many present, however, proclaimed the great efficacy of cures suggested by this miracle man. We also heard of him using his miraculous powers to get the daughter of a rich widow married into a princely family, a match the boy had earlier rejected. This marriage ended in a disaster, however, since the mother of the girl was charged with stealing a necklace during the wedding and there was a great deal of unpleasantness for all concerned.

I came back with the impression of having witnessed a magician's performance. Can anything of this nature ever be satisfying to the soul?

India is full of similar strange occurrences, particularly in the hill areas. Simple folk are most impressionable and it is these men and women that some spirits use most often as their mediums, who, once vacated by the spirit, are left a wreck. These people are so constituted that, once a spirit has formed an attraction to them, they are unable to resist. The medium is hardly the kind of person who can make an effective contribution towards spiritual evolution, as there is no guarantee that the spirit using the medium, deserves respect, or is merely a conjuror.

# 5

# Deities and Gurus
# in the Hills

The hill areas of Himachal Pradesh in India abound in village and clan deities. The temples housing these deities are tended by priests who are, in most cases, Mediums for the spirits they worship, in addition to which they act as Gurus or guides to the local population. Any kind of mundane problem is taken to them at all hours of the day and night, along with the appropriate fee, whereupon the spirit of the local deity enters their body and they begin answering the questions put to them. Men and women bow to them again and again, ask forgiveness for their past sins and guidance for the future.

On one occasion I arrived in a remote village which is about 14,000 feet above sea level and depends mostly on sheep farming for its livelihood. The villagers grew barley and a few potatoes, assisted by an abundant supply of water, and although they were very poor, they had a magnificent temple to a 'naag' or cobra deity. On the day of my arrival, there was a festival and the image of the deity was to be taken out in a palanquin supported by two strong thick bamboos held by eight men. The image itself could not have weighed more than ten kilos, and I therefore could not understand why eight men were needed to support it. They explained, 'When the deity enters the image in accordance with their prayers, it grows very heavy and starts swinging of its own accord. This swing is so strong that eight men can hardly support the deity as it moves in this weird fashion.' I was introduced to the priest, and the village elders asked me if I would like to question the deity, at a price. As I was keen to see the whole process, I agreed.

The deity was brought out of the temple with traditional respect and put in the palanquin. Eight sturdy men had volunteered to carry it and the torch-light procession moved off through the village with all the villagers following behind. It was an impressive sight.

I remained in attendance, close to the priest. Soon after the march commenced, the palanquin began to jerk, first slowly, then vigorously. I felt the bamboo pole to test the strength of the swing; it was in fact, very powerful. I did not think I could control this swing movement; at first, I thought that the bamboo poles were the cause. But the bamboos could not by themselves, have made the palanquin swing from side to side in such a pronounced manner. At this moment, I noticed that the priest was getting into some kind of fit and the village headmen started imploring the deity in him to speak out. My questions were put to this pandit, who was now in a sort of trance, and he answered them most vaguely. To me, even the trance appeared unreal. On further pleading by the village headmen, the pandit or rather the spirit occupying the pandit's body, asked me to make a representation on behalf of the village to the central Government, of which I was a high official. This I did, as I had promised, though, to what effect, I do not know.

I noticed that the villagers were superstitious and this kind of deity worship had contributed nothing but fear to their lives. Fear of the unknown makes men hesitant to take any initiative in their lives. The pandit had made himself all-powerful and an object of fear, and never before had I come across such spiritual degredation. Spiritual life should always be elevating, and should eradicate fear and make people self-reliant. It is better for a man to be a non-believer than to have a belief which cripples him and turns him into a beggar.

# 6

# The 'Crystal Gazing' Gurus

One cannot help being impressed by the spiritual powers of an individual who can accurately foretell the future. We have many such astrologers in our country who are highly respected and many of whom have amassed immense wealth. There are some who follow the Bhrigu Sanhita, a compilation of the works, which the great rishi Bhrigu is supposed to have left, thousands of years ago, to help guide the material life of some great souls, in the interest of their evolution. This exhaustive literature appears to have been extensively copied and expanded during the time of Akbar the Great. Hence, one finds many pandits who have bundles of these old parchments and read out your future if they happen to possess your horoscope. A reading I had done by a pandit in Jullundar in the Punjab proved to be quite accurate. On my next visit to this town ten years later, the old man had retired, after building a few modern houses, and his sons were too busy roaming about on scooters to be bothered any more. But you could go to almost any town in India and you would meet a 'Bhrigu' pandit, though I am sure a large number are not genuine.

Then, there are other pandits, particularly in the South, who are called Nadi astrologers. One at Bangalore, after studying my thumb with a powerful lense for a while, produced a bundle of split reeds on which were etched the futures of various horoscopes. His reading was also fairly accurate. There are, in addition, hundreds of good palmists, some reputedly fabulously wealthy, whose predictions are remarkably accurate. Casting horoscopes, hand-reading and crystal gazing is done quite extensively in the West, and some Indian experts like Cheiro have acquired world renown.

I myself, however, have come across some astounding men

31

who could answer your queries without your saying a thing, literally quoting the wording of your questions which you are invited to write on a paper and then conceal. In one place, the pandit turned to me and said, 'You are asking this question on behalf of your daughter, who in turn, is asking questions on your behalf.' This was absolutely true and his prediction, for which he charged nothing, proved right.

Another pandit correctly guessed questions and their sequence and produced the right answer, except in one case where the date was wrong. One actually took money while another asked us to give our contribution to a religious society of which he was a distinguished official. I have had my hand read by a doctor and a service man without any fee and with a fair degree of accuracy.

I was so fascinated with this subject that I saw almost anyone who was reputed to be good. My main reason was to find out if the whole of a man's life was pre-planned or pre-ordained. Was there a pattern of some sort in life? What is the nature and extent of free-will in a person's life? I am coming to the conclusion that there is a definite design in my own life at least. This life-pattern unfolds itself with time, and even apparently meaningless events—for example childhood pranks—assume their proper place in the divine design. Freewill is without a doubt, incorporated in the life-pattern. The place, and date and time of birth is no accident; nor are the circumstances of birth. Similarly relatives, friends and enemies are no accident. They are a part of an extremely well thought-out design in which successes and failures are neither accidents nor the direct result of personal endeavour. In everything we do, we are governed by our nature which is formed by the powerful urges and unfulfilled desires of the past birth, joining hands with the seed and circumstances of the present one.

No one can remain, even for a moment, without doing work; everyone is made to act helplessly by the impulses born of nature.
*Shrimad Bhagwad Gita*

Nature acts as the perpetual source of will so that the lazy and the active, evil-doers as well as saints, are an essential part of the grand design and each acts according to his nature.

Once a saint was sitting in complete peace on the bank of a river, when he saw a scorpion being drowned by a wave. He at once put his hand in the water and lifted the scorpion in an attempt to take it out of the water. Hardly had he touched the scorpion when it stung him most viciously. The pain of the sting made the saint drop the animal back into the water. But then he again saw it drown and he could not help putting his hand again in the water to save its life. The scorpion stung him again and he was forced to drop it back into the water once more. Twice stung, the saint still could not resist the temptation of saving the animal's life. Once again, he put his hand into the water and threw the scorpion out of the water at the cost of a third sting.

A man who was watching this incident could not help asking the saint the reasons for his foolhardy act to save the life of an ungrateful and vicious creature. The saint replied, 'The scorpion cannot forsake his nature nor can I. All of us are slaves of our nature.'

This is the reason why a horoscope, which is the chart of our nature and its potential made at the time of birth, can foretell the future life of an individual with remarkable accuracy, depending upon the knowledge and experience of the astrologer. The lines on the hand generally corroborate the horoscope. There are also some lines or indications on the forehead of an individual which depict his future.

A further, more evolved practice exists, at which some saints and sadhus excel, for which it is not necessary to examine an individual's head or horoscope to know all about his life.

A Muslim faqir of about forty-five years of age used to visit our Sikh house, almost annually. He would knock on the door and come in when the door was opened, usually by my mother, who would welcome any sadhu. He would be bare-headed and bare-footed, wearing only a shirt and silvar, or loose kind of trousers. He would say, 'Daughter, get me one-and-a-half chapaties.' My mother would quickly bring them, whereupon he would sit on the floor behind the door, eat them with relish and disappear for another year. On one such occasion, he told my mother that I would be coming home after a month (I was then involved in the war in Burma) and that she would write to me to bring a blanket for him. My mother knew I was in the war on active service and there was no likelihood of my coming home in a month. So, she took no action on this request of the faqir for whom she had great respect. One of my cousins, who had lost her husband some years before, asked this faqir, when she would receive a letter from her husband.

The faqir, without even looking at her, said, 'Child, has anyone ever received letters from the land of the dead? Why do you ridicule a poor man in this manner?' My cousin was greatly impressed by the clairvoyance possessed by this unusual faqir.

Reverting to my own story, I was suddenly sent for by my senior commander, who had seen me working hard under the great stress of War. He said, 'You can have a free ride to India by an Air Force plane for a short holiday at home.' I was delighted and arrived home unexpectedly. My mother was amazed and full of joy, and told me how the faqir had predicted my return home after a month and here I was, exactly as foretold. The surprising point was the faqir turned up on the same day, despite the fact that he normally visited us only once a year and had been to our house only a month before. Immediately on arrival he asked for my blanket. We all felt ashamed at not having believed him. In those days a blanket cost very little and he would not accept any money. And as he just wanted a blanket from me, I ran to the bazaar and purchased one for him. All his predictions have come true except one. He said that I would acquire land one day and he would then ask me for a plot in it for his grave so that I could ensure its respect and maintenance. It is about thirty years since I met him last when he was in Rawalpindi, and the country has since been partitioned. I have purchased some land and would be delighted to serve him for the rest of his life if he turned up again and I like to think he will, not because his predictions were correct, but because his life was a model for many of us to follow.

Another Moslem faqir in my village, who was a Sayyad called Akbar Shah, roamed about naked in the village, and spent nights in the grave-yards or cremation grounds and ate

34

pieces of mud, munching them as if they were sweets. He was bleary-eyed and always inebriated with God's name. 'Allah huh', 'Allah huh' would be heard wherever Akbar Shah was. Once in a while he would come to my father-in-law's house where my mother-in-law, who was a great Sikh devotee of God, would give him oven-baked loaves to eat. He would enjoy them and say, 'Mad woman! Do not worry about your daughter; she will be well-married.' Everything he said came true. The only other house he would visit besides my father-in-law's was that of a Moslem carpenter. There he would lie for hours, as if dead. He was a subject of ridicule for the urchins, but those who knew his powers, literally worshipped him. After the death of my mother-in-law, he just disappeared and no one ever saw him again in our village.

I witnessed an event which I find hard to imagine. A sick woman, one of Baba Onkarnath's devotees, was presented to him, whom he touched on the forehead. As a result of this and his unique powers, she had visions of saints, gods and goddesses who spoke to her and gave her guidance on the day-to-day problems of life. These visions would occur several times a day, during which she appeared to be dozing yet was fully conscious.

She would doze off in her sickness and see a beautiful girl come up with a tumbler full of some kind of elixir and touch the tumbler to her lips. She would soon recover and her temperature would go down. The sick woman would be told about what medicines to take. This was something much more than simply knowing the future, it carried the remedies to all problems. This lady saw Hanivan, playing his part in a war, in which I too was engaged. If she thought of any of her children, she would at once see them in their far-off stations, and could describe the clothes they were wearing and exactly what they were doing. Praying to Baba Onkarnath, she would even resolve their problems.

Once she saw the wife of Mr Lio Shao Chi sobbing; she described her beautiful long neck, her green dress and Chinese features. A few days later, we heard that Lio Shao Chi had been deprived of his authority and was in disgrace. She saw the wife of Mr Kruschev in tears and Kruschev in a tearing rage.

35

The amazing point here was that she had never seen these people or even their photographs and although she may have heard their names on the radio, at the time when she saw the visions, no news about these events had yet percolated through to the rest of the world.

Were these noble women she saw in her visions true believers in God despite being married to staunch Communists? Only the future can disclose this secret. They appeared to be on the same spiritual wavelength and hence able to communicate their pain to this gifted lady. She saw the deaths of some prominent men in whom I was interested, and in some cases saw their new births also.

The new births proved in every case the justice of the powers that govern the cycle of rebirth. Baba advised her not to disclose them to anyone. All one can say today with conviction is that good deeds, and an honest, loving heart do have their reward, just as evil acts have their punishments. Sincere prayers are also heard and promptly answered, and the angels will arrive to console you in your sorrow just as they did in the case of this lady.

They are not dreams, they are real occurrences, since whatever happens, has a meaning, and the advice given by these super-minds is always true and useful.. On one such occasion, Swami Vivekananda, wearing typical pagri or headgear, came to offer advice concerning something overseas. On another occasion, Hanuman Ji, the Bannar Prince, who led the forces of Lord Rama against King Ravana, gave darshan and this lady saw me in military uniform holding a rifle and battle axe. By these signs, we concluded that the war was coming and I would be participating in it. That was about six months before the Bangladesh war.

She saw Sheikh Mujib Rahman coming out of a jailroom wearing shirt and loose trousers, and saw his toothbrush and other personal effects being packed. Later, she saw him boarding an aircraft in very dim light, though we were not sure whether this meant his transfer to another country or his release from jail. She again prayed for his release, so that he could meet his family, and later saw him meeting his youngest son, Russel. This lady had never met either of them. But, we were now certain that he would be released and fly to his own country to be reunited with his family. The meeting with Russel must have been as emotional as seen in this vision.

She is certain that her guru, Baba Onkarnath arranged all this because of his kindness so that now she is never without hope; her devotion to God and her guru increases by leaps and bounds. This, naturally, influences the rest of the family, and everyone is now convinced about the advantages of surrendering to God and guru.

One could go on describing these visions indefinitely since they are so numerous, and all true. They are sights of such indescribable beauty that the lady in question says they cannot be compared with anything known in this world and hence cannot be named. Are these visions of other worlds, on seeing which an individual loses all taste for the sights of this world and so becomes merged with God? Does anyone know of a greater miracle than this? Can there be any doubt about the existence of God, faith in Whom can alone bring forth such experiences? Can there be any doubt about the spiritual level of someone who can change a man or woman into a god by mere touch?

> Who turned humans into gods in the twinkling of an eye
> *Guru Granth Sahib*

It is clear to us that even ordinary people can be given powers of clairvoyance beyond those possessed by some gurus. Clairvoyance is not the only qualification for a spiritual guru. Otherwise, all crystal gazers would fall into that category.

# 7

## *Seances*

Spiritualism in the West mostly means communication with the spirits of those who have died and is mainly done for personal benefit and often for material gain. Usually dead relatives are invited to contact a medium and answer questions. A planchette, a small board supported by two castors, is set up with a pencil held in a vertical position, which traces marks on the paper, without a conscious effort of a hand holding the pencil. The International Society for Physical Research has enough data to prove that the intelligent ego which occupies the body during its life time, does not die when the body dies. If its merit does not allow it to travel above the sub-astral spheres, it remains in the magnetic fields close to the earth and awaits re-birth. These spirits do not improve their wisdom or character upon death and can be contacted through a medium. There are some evil spirits who greatly enjoy attaching themselves to mediums and ruining their moral and material life. Lower spirits which provide information by planchette, are themselves in need of advice. Leave them alone to work out their own salvation, as there are Masters also responsible for that task. They are born as Masters and speak with knowledge and authority or come in clear visions to devotees and in this way guide them. In this field of spiritualism, there is little chance of detecting any fraud by evil and designing spirits until it is too late, and I have come across some excellent men who have fallen victims to such fraud and have completely ruined themselves. The novelty of the experience of a seance attracts a large number of innocent men and women.

Spiritualism has become a religion to some in the West, where spiritualists have built their own churches and appointed their own Ministers. They usually pick simple souls as mediums and do not think about the consequences of such an evil practice, particularly on the Medium.

There is the tantric cult in India of a similar kind, though slightly more advanced. Its exponents also use spirits for evil ends and invariably come to grief themselves. They are some of the most depraved men of this universe, staying near cremation grounds and indulging in an orgy of vice. Some of them advocate human sacrifices for material gains, while others recite mantras to harm their enemies or to enrich themselves and their friends. They do not follow the real tantric philosophy of repeating God's name which is the best elixir for all castes and communities. This is mentioned here since many people fall prey to the designs of these scheming individuals and never recover from the spiritual setback.

God, in his mercy, recently made me a witness to a seance session. The man responsible for calling the spirit into his house did not himself believe in spiritualism. Circumstances, however, induced him to use any means to acquire some information about his son who was a major in the Army and was reported dead during the Indo-Pakistan War of 1971, a report he refused to believe. He told the Commanding Officer of his son's battalion that the certificate confirming the death of his son in the military hospital, from shell wounds, was false and the man it referred to was not his son. The helmet sent to him as an article of sentimental value was several sizes too big for his son. Actually, nothing of genuine sentimental value was recovered or sent to him. None of his son's personal possessions—watch, identity disc, keys or anything else—was found. The father is a committed yogi, who teaches yoga as a cure for various diseases of the body for reasonable fees. This brought him into contact with some European Red Cross officers of the UNO, one of whom did locate his son's name and number in the list of wounded Indians in a Pakistani military hospital, and informed the father of this fact by letter from New York. This confirmed the father's conviction that his son was alive and was not shown in the POW list by the Pakistan authorities, due to reasons best known to themselves. About three hundred Indian officers and other ranks were listed as missing by the Indian authorities, but Pakistan had

39

denied any knowledge of them also.

This yogi then went to all the saints and sadhus as well as astrologers and tantrics, each one of whom told him his son was alive and would return home one day. The Indian Army authorities, however, were not prepared to contradict the evidence of the hospital letter stating that the man had died, and that after cremation, his personal effects as found on his body, were despatched to the army unit concerned, which, in turn had sent them all to this yogi. No one in authority would ever admit that a mistake fould have been made in the identity of a wounded man brought in on a stretcher soaked with blood. Even the cards put on stretchers to show various particulars could have been changed. The yogi was restless. His friend in the United Nations promised to get a letter for him as proof of his existence, but it was bound to take time.

Ultimately, during a seance, he was introduced to a spirit, who introduced himself as a high soul. The yogi converted one of his bedrooms into a well-decorated temple, with images and photographs of Lord Rama, Lord Krishna Ma Durga and Hanumanji, as directed by this spirit, and he started daily sessions in his own house. A small stove was used as a planchette, the two legs being supported by the yogi's second son, with two fingers to each leg, while the burner was held lightly and kept from tilting by the yogi's wife. One leg of the stove wrote on the floor on which some flour was spread so that the writing would show.

This spirit now lives permanently in this room, and after prayers, on the stove being touched, vibrations indicate that the spirit has possessed the stove. Questions put to the spirit are answered in writing, mostly in Hindi. The writing is faster than the most practised scribe could achieve, and the sense more lucid. The spirit begins with pooja or worship of deities in the room; then follows a distribution of fruits, initially brought into the room by the yogi.

According to the yogi, the spirit has explained the Hindu philosophy of evolution, with special emphasis on love of God. An explanation was also given of the word AUM, as denoting the three worlds, Akash, Mritya and Patal Lok, with the Sun and Moon as sustainers of this universe.

This spirit confirmed to the yogi again and again that his son was alive and would return home before next Janmashtmi, or Lord Krishna's Birthday. He authenticated it by saying 'this is the promise or vachen of Lord Rama'. Often he would describe the yogi's son's clothes, his companions, the food they were eating, and the conversation between his son and the sentry guarding them. The meal one day included three chapaties, one small dish of rice, dal and vegetables. There were four prisoners in one room, all wearing bluish Mazri cloth shirts and trousers. The spirit named the exact place where they were secretly confined by the Pakistan army. He said they had been given the English translation of the Koran to study, with the obvious aim of converting them to Islam.

The spirit has mentioned in my presence that there were eleven air force officers similarly confined at Larkana, Mr Bhutto's home-town in Sind. They may be some of those reported missing or even dead, like the yogi's son. At the time of writing this book the Yogi's son has not been returned to India, but, I feel confident that the good Moslems in Pakistan amongst them will never tolerate this situation when they come to know of it, and perhaps the release of these innocent soldiers would generate true goodwill towards Pakistan in India. The time, therefore, cannot be far off when some true Moslem will take charge and transform the whole atmosphere of the Indian sub-continent.

This yogi who became known to me through a mutual friend, held my opinion in such esteem that he said he would only believe in this spirit if I would approve of it after a session Although I am personally against the whole system of spiritualism, which is full of many dangers, I had, perforce, to attend a couple of sessions to help my yogi friend in search of truth.

During my first session, the 'spirit in the stove', for the first time wrote its sermon in Gurmukhi, a punjabi script, which I could read and, fortunately, the yogi's second son, though out of practice, could also read. First the spirit wrote the words, ek onkar, and explained the meaning. Then it wrote 'Waheguru' in Gurmukhi and again explained the meaning. He said 'you praise someone who does something unique, something wonderful, and you say "Wah". What could be a great wonder than the creation of Universe by God. So you say "Wah". God alone therefore is worthy of such praise and is addressed as "Wahe Guru".'

We then went on to various mundane questions and answers, to which the spirit said that the future held great successes in its womb and was pleasing. Then it asked us to wait for seventeen minutes and do bhajan while it would travel to see the yogi's prisoner son. Exactly on time there was vibration in the stove and the spirit wrote that on the way to the prisoner, who was safe, it had to save a lamb kid from drowning in a river. It said it was raining hard in that part of Pakistan. The Yogi's son and his prisoner companions were talking of their families left in India and were well though somewhat downhearted.

I then asked the spirit if it would tell me something about the spirit world which I could use for the benefit of our world. It said it would, and we fixed 4 p.m. the next day for this purpose. Incidentally, during this session, the spirit asked me to show it the palm of my right hand for reading, and asked me to remove the second ring I was wearing, which it considered harmful. It also made astrological diagrams, just like an astrologer does before he reads your future, which showed it to be knowledgeable in this subject. On my arrival the next day, the spirit gave fruit as prasad to me, then asked me to describe in Hindi the name of the book which I intended to write, and for which I was seeking a message from the spirit. When I had given the title, the spirit asked me to describe the contents, which I did.

When I talked of sadhus performing miracles, it said, Do you believe in these miracle men, who acquire deivi siddhis and call themselves gods?' 'No', I replied. It said 'Only God performs true miracles. I respect your faith in the essence of religion and not in miracles'.

When I talked of Baba Sita Ram Das Onkarnath as my guru, it said, 'If you wish to gain moksha, hold fast to the apron-strings of this great soul, Sat Chit Anand, who will fill you with truth and joy so you will achieve salvation while still alive.'

At this point the spirit began describing the scientific meaning of the names of God, which Indian rishis compósed, with a view to attaining awareness of God. It said that the letters were chosen scientifically, since their intonation causes vibrations which affect the body, the mind and the soul. There is unimaginable power behind the combination of certain letters, which removes the lack of balance between the mind and the body, making the body healthy and the mind steady and aware of God. The utterance of these words, which, when given by a guru, become potencized gurmantras, lights up the path as well as clears the way towards the goal of complete devotion to God. Examples of such words are 'Rama' and 'Krishna' and the many other words used as names of God. The spirit particularly expressed the value of the name Rama; which was composed of the letters 'Ra' and 'Ma'. 'Ra' effects the hridaya or heart; then rises to the forehead and coupled with 'Ma', it forms Rama, which affects the atma or soul. Utterance of the word Rama with closed eyes and deep concentration cleanses the body and the mind, making both healthy. It removes all imbalances and makes an awareness of God possible.

When I asked the spirit if it was true that higher spirits never communicate with this world by means of a seance, it said that spirits like himself required much devotion and imprecation before they came to help people, as in the present case. Mostly, it was the lower spirits that came.

I said, 'I have heard stories of mediums and others who indulge in this practice being considerably harmed as a result.' It said, 'Yes, lower spirits do get annoyed by being disturbed, and some even take delight in causing damage. In any case, when spirits are called for selfish ends, those that answer the call also respond selfishly. You are lighting a fire for a selfish purpose.'

I said, 'What happens to a man when he dies?' The spirit said, 'Some achieve the salvation which may have taken them several births. Some get born again. Many wait for rebirth for varying periods. Some bad people become 'prets' or evil spirits, and may never get a chance of rising higher on the ladder of evolution; they remain almost condemned for all time.

When asked if there was any company for the dead people awaiting rebirth, the spirit said, 'No, they remain alone. Sometimes, they may meet some friends or relatives of similar status, but mostly they remain alone and helpless.'

I said, 'A satguru is supposed to keep the company of his disciples during and after death. Can the guru not help these lonely souls? The spirit said, 'It is the guru's wish. The satguru can do whatever he likes. There are no Masters to help these souls while they await birth. Masters are found in your world, not here. Only unsatisfied souls meet here and no one can help anyone else even if he is a relative or a friend.' The spirit also said that the soul of a departed person will stay at the place of death for seven days, after which it will leave the place of death. Nam Kirtan helps the soul as well as those who are left behind, and Shardh or feasting of pandits on specified days, helps those not yet born. Since no one knows when dead relatives have been re-born or not, it is customary to continue doing Shardh.

I had spent a lot of time with the yogi and many questions remained unexplored, despite the fact that the spirit was willing to tell all. For my purposes, however, I had learnt enough. The predictions will take time to be proved right, though I am not convinced of the truth of all that was said by the spirit. What is certain is that the guru or Master is a great help here and in the hereafter; that God's name as given by the saint-guru as a potencized mantra is the key to being aware of the essence of God; that man has higher purposes than mere existence and procreation.

We have created man in the best mould
*The Holy Koran 95:4*

This spirit finally said that I should reproduce the picture of a lotus flower, which represents the soul, for my book, with its two broad green leaves resting on the surface of water representing a balanced state of body and mind. It further gave the following message: 'If any one of these two green leaves, the body and the mind, is agitated for some reason or gets damaged, the balance is disturbed and the lotus flower itself loses its lustre. Devout religious people, though obtaining sustenance from the mud of sansara or world of illusion, transcend it and shine forth like the lotus.'

All those who read this book with devotion, renouncing attachment and anger and imbibing the truths enunciated within the book, shall become like the lotus.

*Agyat (Unknown)*

# 8

# A Christian Saint

Verily I say unto you, if ye have faith, and dount not if ye shall say unto this mountain, Be thou removed, and be thou cast into the Sea; it shall be done.

*Jesus Christ*

Shri Yogananda, in his *Autobiography of a Yogi,* has mentioned two Christian saints. The first is Luther Burbank (died in 1926), an American scientist who proved the value of love in producing higher varieties of plants, such as the thornless cactus. He would talk to plants and affectionately assure them of his love and care for them. He would ask those cacti to shed their defensive thorns since he himself was there to protect them, and in course of time, he evolved a thornless variety. His utter sincerity and honesty of purpose and child-like simplicity made a deep impact on Swami Yogananda who taught him the techniques of Kriya Yoga. Luther Burbank, who also greatly impressed Hazrat, told Swamji many stories of his healing sick people as well as plants by love. The name 'Burbank' is now listed in the Websters International Dictionary and, as a transitive verb, it means 'To cross or graft a plant.' Hence, figuratively, to improve anything, as a process or institution by selecting good features and rejecting bad, or by adding good features.

In this connection it is interesting to quote Luther Burbank's views on the future of humanity: 'I see humanity as one enormous plant, which for its development needs love, the natural blessing of much open air and a sensible selection when marrying. In my own life I have seen such remarkable progress in the development of plants that I look forward with optimism to a healthy, happy world as soon as its children will be educated in the principles of a simple, sensible life. We must return to nature and to the God of nature.

I am protesting against the educational systems of today, separated from nature and suffocating the development of the individual.

The orient possesses immeasurable treasures of knowledge, which the Western world is only now starting to discover.

The other saint mentioned by Shri Yogananda is Therese Neumann, the Catholic Stigmatist of Bavaria. Injured in an accident at the age of twenty, she had become blind and paralysed, but by praying to St Teresa, she regained her sight and power in her limbs. For years, she ate nothing except a consecrated wafer. Every Friday the Stigmata—the sacred wounds of Christ—appeared on her head, breast, hands and feet and she suffered in her body all the agonies Christ went through. Swamiji himself not only saw these wounds oozing bloody, but, on inducing a trance through yoga techniques, was himself able to see the vision of Christ and the agony He was suffering, just as she was experiencing them in her body.

I have often heard of Christian men and women of tremendous faith who, through the strength of their character, changed the very outlook of all who came in contact with them.

But the memory of one is so outstanding that it is impossible to forget it. Once, I had a farm in the Terai area in the foothills of the Himalayas, where I used to go and stay for several days. It was a jungle area which was thrown open to the refugees coming from West-Pakistan in the wake of disturbances during the partition of India in 1947. Terai is well-known for its malarial mosquitoes, wild elephants and tigers. Being virgin soil, the land was fertile but had to be brought under cultivation by cutting away the jungle, burning the roots of trees and tilling the ground with tractors. It was a tough life, full of hazards, which attracted some very rough characters from across the border, some of whom came from notoriously criminal tribes whose main occupation before partition was stealing horses, buffaloes and cows, and then selling them. They were fleet-footed and good horsemen, and were land-hungry and grabbed hold of any part of territory that they could lay their hands on, both legally as well as illegally. The gentlemen farmers from the Punjab and absentee landlords found these tough characters nibbling away at their land without any fear of consequences.

Acting in the capacity as honourary Secretary to a Soldiers' Society, I noticed during one of my visits, that one such neighbour was busy ploughing land, clearly marked as being ours, which he claimed belonged to him. Only on discovering we were soldiers, and armed, did he vacate this land he had illegally claimed to own.

The poverty and misery in this area had attracted a Christian missionary, who also wished to help with relief work and to further this end, he had purchased some land and was planning to build a Church and a relief centre. His close neighbour was one of those criminals, who tried to frighten the missionary out of this area so that he could also occupy his land. One day, at about 3 p.m. when the missionary was walking alone in a jungle close to his land, he was caught by this character, tied to a tree and given a severe beating, and was told to leave the area if he wanted to stay alive. The missionary became unconscious after this beating, but later was seen by a passerby who untied the ropes and took him to the hospital where he recovered.

Everyone told him to report the serious assault by this bad character to the police, which he refused to do. Instead he told the hospital authorities and other sympathizers who were themselves fed up with the objectionable and criminal activities of his tormentor, 'Why should I report to the police when He himself was there and is a witness to all that happened.' They asked him to name the person to whom he was referring. He said, 'God Himself. He is everywhere; He watches everything and it is His function to do justice. He is impartial. I am engaged in His work. Why should I go and report to the Police?'

Everyone was amazed at the faith this remarkable missionary had in God. No one had come across such faith under such circumstances. But while everyone appreciated his faith, they could not understand how this matter would ultimately be resolved. The notorious character had already successfully thrown out some faint-hearted neighbours. He would regularly get drunk and beat up someone or other. The law seemed to be helpless against this desperado.

The next day the missionary was again tied by him to a tree and given an even more severe thrashing. Again, someone released him and took him to the hospital. Now the people insisted that he should report to the authorities. But the missionary appeared more determined than ever to leave this affair to the justice of the Lord.

Then something happened which even a child of that area will recite to you if you mention this subject. It was the clearest proof that God is omnipresent and is just and protects His loved ones. He may test your faith rather sternly but He compensates you for it in the end.

The notorious character got into a brawl with an equally bad character over a trifling matter. His opponent this time was not only powerful, but resolute and swore that he would tie this man to a tree and beat him senseless daily, till he changed his habits and became a God-fearing citizen. For several days, people would watch this man drag the criminal to a lonely spot, tie him to a tree and beat him mercilessly till he himself got tired and left him unconscious till the next day. After a few such experiences, the man begged for mercy and was excused.

That very day, a murdered body was found buried in his fields and the police took him into custody. Some people say that he had nothing to do with that murder and that some of his many enemies had buried the body in his fields to take revenge on him. The police in those days were very tough and used to force to get to the truth, and it is said that he used to get beaten daily by the police. The strangest thing was that his beatings would always start at about 3 p.m., so that he could connect the two incidents.

People flocked to the Christian Missionary and he became the most respected man of God in the Terai forest area, though much to my regret, I have forgotten the name and address of this Christian Saint. The incident took place some twenty-five years ago and I have not been there now for about twenty years, but I am informed by a friend that people of that area still remember this unusual miracle of the Christian Saint.

49

# 9

## *Sufi Saints*

The spread of Islam may have followed in the wake of the victorious and zealous Moslem armies, but it was nurtured and sustained by the great Sufi saints. Sufism, the mystical cult within Islam which follows the Master-Disciple or Guru-Chela discipline of spiritual evolution, is said to have been founded by the followers of Hazrat Ali, son-in-law of and successor to the Prophet Muhammad. The Master is called Murshid, or Pir or Shaikh-ul-Mashaikh or Pir-o-Murshid and the initiate has to make a total surrender to his Master, who then enlightens his disciple spiritually. Contemplation, meditation and constant living with God are essential parts of the Sufi spiritual practice, while poetry and devotional music form a basic complement of their philosophy. Some of the most sensitive and touching poetry ever written has been produced by Sufi saints, such as Moulana Jelaluddin Rumi and Hafiz, and Sufi devotional music or qawwalis is equally beautiful and exhilerating, and can induce a state of trance and spiritual elevation known as 'wajad'.

Sufi saints are open-hearted and liberal-minded, giving due respect to every religion on earth which, together with their exemplary devotion to God, attracts thousands of followers from all religious denominations. Sikh gurus like Guru Nanak were so impressed by the similarity of their own and Sufi philosophy that the poetry of these Moslem Sufi saints was included in the Sikh religious scripture, as in the case of Guru Granth Sahib, and given equal status as an object of worship. It is less of a surprise, therefore, that the foundation stone of the Sikh Golden Temple at Amritsar was laid by a Moslem Sufi saint, Sai Mian Mir.

The Chishti order of Sufis, founded in Iran, produced some of the most famous Sufi saints in India. Amongst them were

50

Khwaja Muinuddin Chishti of Ajmer, often called Gharib Navaz or 'Cherisher of the Poor'; and Khwaja Qutubuddin Bakhtyar Kaki of Delhi, in whose memory, King Eltutomush Tughlat is said to have built the famous Qutub Minar at Delhi. After him came Sheikh Baba Farid, 'Ganj Shakar or Storehouse of Sugar, and his renowned disciple Sheikh Nizamuddin Aulia Mehboob-e-Ilahi, Beloved of God, of Delhi.

Sheikh Baba Farid lived a householder's life and spoke to the people of Punjab, both Hindus and Moslems alike, in their own language, Punjabi. Some of his Punjabi verses have become a part of folklore. Many miracles are also associated with Sheikh Baba Farid's name. The fanatic qazi of Ajodhan accused Farid of un-Islamic practices, like singing and dancing in utter disregard of the Shariah, the Moslem law. When the emperor paid no attention to this accusation, since he knew how sincere Farid's faith was, the Qazi hired some assassins to kill Farid, an attempt which failed. Later, the Qazi gave his daughter in marriage to Farid's third son, Badruddin Sulaiman.

It is said Baba Farid lived for twelve years without any food. Once he was drafted into forced labour during which his load, a basket of mud, was seen floating in the air above his head to everyone's amazement. Baba Farid insisted on the observance of Moslem law, but later Sufis were more liberal. Sheikh Farid, while insisting on visiting the mosque five times a day for prayers, said God neither dwells in the heavens nor in forests but is enthroned in the heart of man.

One of his lovely poems runs:

Farid, why wanderest thou over wild places,
Trampling thorns under thy feet?
God abides in the heart: seek him not in lonely waste

Baba Farid's great-grandfather, Farrukh Shah of Kabul, was a descendant of the Caliph Hazrat Omar, but was profoundly influenced by his mother, who was a direct descendant of Hazrat Ali. Greatly impressed by the piety and charm of Hazrat Syed Qutubuddin Bakhtyar Kaki, Baba Farid became his disciple and was also blessed by Khwaja Muinuddin Ajmeri. Thousands followed him when he

51

succeeded his Master on his death. He lived a simple life, spurning favours and presents from kings. His Sikh admirers built an altar where a gurdwara or Sikh temple and a mosque stand side by side in the town of Faridkot in the Punjab, named after Baba Farid.

Baba Farid was succeeded by his eminent disciple Sheikh Nizamuddin Aulia, who was known as 'Mehboob-e-Ilahi', the Beloved of God. Seven kings ruled during the hundred years of this saint's life though he never met any of them. One king, however, Ghiasuddin Tughlaq, was adamant that the Sufi saint pay him homage. While on his way to Delhi after a victory in Bengal, he sent word that if the Saint did not present himself for obeisance on his arrival at Delhi, he would be punished to set an example. Hazrat Nizamuddin Aulia merely replied, 'As yet, Delhi is far off'. Tughlaq died before reaching Delhi.

One of Hazrat Nizamuddin Aulia's most famous disciples was Amir Khusro, the court poet. Credited with being the originator of the Urdu language, he was also an eminent Persian scholar and wrote excellent poetry in Hindi. As a disciple, many considered him ideal; in the daytime he would be in the Royal Courts, and at night, he would go to his Master, Nizamuddin Aulia, to whom he would recite his new poems as a lullaby, and then would go to sleep on the floor at his feet.

It is said a poor man once came to seek some financial help for his daughter's marriage from Nizamuddin Aulia, who had no money at hand. Instead, he gave a pair of his old shoes to the poor man, saying, 'This is all I have'. The man picked up the smelly old shoes, tied them in his cloth and started on his way home, cursing his luck. He halted at an inn on the way, where, by chance, Amir Khusro was also staying, who, smelling the scent of his master coming from the old shoes, set about finding whether someone had come from Delhi after meeting Nizamuddin Aulia. Finally, he found the poor man, who admitted meeting Nizamuddin Aulia, but lamented that all he had got from him was the smelly old shoes, instead of the money for which he had gone to him. Amir Khusro picked up his master's shoes, kissed them over and over again, and said,

'I was wondering what it was of my master's that I smelt.' He then humbly offered the poor man all his possessions including several camel-loads of rich goods which he had with him, in exchange for Nizamuddin Aulia's shoes. Only then did the poor man realize what an expensive present the master had concealed in such unassuming poverty.

On reaching Delhi Amir Khusro informed his master of this incident, and how he had purchased his old shoes, to which the master said, 'You got them very cheaply.'

When Khusro heard of the death of his Master, he travelled hundreds of miles to reach Delhi. The Master had said before his death, 'Do not let Khusro come near my grave otherwise it will burst open to receive him too and this will be against the Moslem law.' Such was the intense love the Master had for his disciple. At one time, Nizamuddin Aulia had said, 'If someone puts a saw on my forehead and asks me either to sacrifice my head or that of my disciple Khusro, I would everytime sacrifice my head but never that of my beloved disciple.'

Khusro, confronted by the grave of his Master found the situation too overwhelming for his soul. He cried aloud for his Master and dropped down dead. Never had people seen such intense affection between a Master and a disciple. Amir Khusro was buried close to his Master and now shares the affection people shower on Nizamuddin Aulia's grave. Pir Zamin Nizami Syed Bukhari, the present Sajjada-e-Nashin, lends great charm and grace to the dargah which thousands of men and women of all creeds still visit today.

Latest in the line of great Sufi saints has been Pir-o-Murshid Hazrat Inayat Khan (1882-1927) who brought Sufism to the West and has many followers all over the world. He travelled widely in America and Europe and wrote several books on Sufism. Of his many books, I have read his book *The Unity of Religious Ideals* again and again. Hazrat Inayat Khan's tomb is near that of Nizamuddin Aulia in Delhi.

For the Sufi, the highest heaven is his own heart. Love is his God. To harmonize with oneself is not enough, thus one must also harmonize with others, which includes the whole world.

Sufism in Arabia gradually adopted a metaphysical attitude towards the interpretation of Islam, whereas in Persia, Sufis stressed the importance of meditation, thus aligning themselves with the mystic traditions already prevalent.

Hazrat Inayat Khan's Murshid, Abu Hashim Madani of Kyderabad, once said, 'There is only one virtue and one sin for a soul on this path: virtue, when he is conscious of God and sin when he is not.'

I live in God-consciousness;
If I forget Him, I die.
*Guru Nanak*

# 10
## Sai Baba of Shirdi

This great saint, whose origin is unknown, used to live in a dilapidated mosque in the village of Shirdi and was loved by both its Moslem and Hindu inhabitants. He did much to relieve the sufferings of the poor, curing their illnesses, removing their mental tensions and inspiring them towards a cleaner and truly religious life. He also performed some remarkable miracles which convinced people of his great spiritual powers. When the local shopkeepers refused to give him oil for lighting his oil lamp, he used ordinary water. It is said that he used to beg his daily food from the village and throw everything thus obtained into a large earthenware pot, to which dogs had access. Thus he shared his meals with animals to show non-believers that God creates and sustains every form of life, and that none is superior to the other. Like Guru Nanak, he was a great uniting force between Hindus and Moslems, and like him, he also lived a simple life dedicated to God and humanity. And as in the case of Guru Nanak, there was a dispute between his Hindu and Moslem devotees over the most fitting way of disposing of his body when he died. In both cases the admirers were able to find an amicable solution which respected the sentiments of both communities.

I was fortunate enough to get hold of his book of miracles, some of which astonished me. He was a great soul and I deeply regretted that his death robbed me of the chance to meet him, though I was determined to go to his samadhi at Shirdi and pay my deep respects to his departed soul.

I felt such a great urge to do this that I took some leave to visit Shirdi. When I arrived, the village was decorated for a festival and hundreds of men and women were praying at the samadhi, which houses a beautiful marble statue of the great saint. I bought the best and costliest flower garlands from a flower stall close by and went inside, praying intensely to Sai Baba to accept my offering and give me an unmistakable sign. As I entered with my garland offering wrapped in a paper, I noticed hundreds of garlands around the neck of the marble statue and hundreds more waiting to be handed over to the priest who would put them around Sai Baba's neck. At this point, the priest stopped taking garlands from the waiting pilgrims, removed those already decking the statue and washed it down. Then, with the marble statue gleamingly clean, the priest asked me, out of all the people in the crowd, to hand over my garland. He put it round the statue's neck and stood back to appreciate the garlanded figure. Tears rolled down my cheeks when I saw this great saint accepting my sincere offering in such a conspicuous manner. I bowed down in utter humility before the statue, and touching its feet with my forehead, I withdrew to a corner and for some time sat in silence. I experienced rare peace in this holy place, knowing Sai Baba's spirit pervaded the samadhi and was guiding seekers of truth, even as he did when he was alive.

## SAI BABA'S MOSLEM DISCIPLE

On learning from a friend that a Moslem disciple of Sai Baba lived near Bombay, I decided to pay him a visit, with someone who knew him well. It was not a day when visitors were entertained but when the identity of the man accompanying me was relayed inside, the gates were opened and we were ushered in. My companion told me that the faqir revealed many truths when in the right mood and that some unscrupulous people, taking advantage of his simplicity, even got from him the numbers of horses which were going to win at the races.

I touched his feet, after which he blessed me and offered tea and then sat by my side on the sofa. To my amazement, he grabbed my hand and put my thumb into his mouth, keeping it there for quite some time. He made one prediction, about my promotion, which came true. He recited the name of Allah continuously and he had a very pleasant personality. Later, I met him a second time in the company with some others and found him charming as before.

# 11
## *Satya Sai Baba*

Except ye see signs and wonders
Ye will not believe

*St John*

I had been very eager to meet Satya Sai Baba ever since I
learnt that he was the reincarnation of Sai Baba of Shirdi.
Satya Baba is famous for his miracles not only in India, but is
also well-known throughout the world. Sai Baba of Shirdi, on
the other hand did not achieve such widespread fame for the
miracles he performed when Sai Baba of Shirdi died, his work
was left incomplete, and, as Great Masters reincarnate several
times, it was inconceivable that such a potent force would not
assume a new body and so continue the task of helping
mankind which had already been started.

From what I heard and read about Satya Baba I had no
doubt that he was a sidha yogi, as his miracles, like those of Sai
Baba of Shirdi, are those of a Master, not a Medium. Shri Sai
Baba of Shirdi could not have reincarnated in a purer or
nobler body than that of Satya Sai Baba. There is a great
resemblance between the powers, mental attitude and
universal love, of both these saints. Their preaching methods
do not differ greatly though the style of the saints does,
necessarily so, since the following of Satya Sai Baba is much
larger, more educated and more widespread. The torn shirt of
the Shirdi style would not be easily recognizable amongst the
scores of thousands that attend the discourses of Satya Sai
Baba and has, therefore, been replaced by a bright red one
which can be seen for miles. Despite the use of all forms of
transport to relay the word of God throughout India and the
rest of the world, it has been found necessary to rely on Satya

Baba's 'fragrance' to refresh those who cannot physically touch him. On occasions such as these, there has to be a public display of miracles, during which Satya Baba uses vibbuti, or sanctified wood-ash, just as Sai Baba used udhi or wood ashes.

Further examples of Shri Satya Baba's miracles may be seen in the surgical operations he performs using astrological instruments, which leave a lasting effect even in educated minds. Images of Lingam, Shiva and Vishnu are produced to strengthen the faith of doubters. Those who consider the production of gold and diamonds as a stronger proof of divinity, are given rings of gold and diamond in an invisible workshop. More advanced disciples are given the darshan of their isht, the highest spiritual entity chosen by the aspirant himself as an ideal for worship by Satya Sai Baba who temporarily assumes that form. Sai Baba of Shirdi did the same in the case of a sceptic who felt revulsion on seeing him cook and eat meat; he assumed the form of Lord Rama who was the isht of this man and immediately removed all his doubts.

All this display of miraculous power is to attract the crowd. The main aim is to awaken the dormant powers of people, totally absorbed in the material world, and make them forget their origin and turn towards their goal, God.

Many great prophets have had to prove their genuine sincerity before people would have faith in their teachings. Before people listen they naturally want some proof, and it is in these situations that miracles play an important role.

When God ordered Moses to lead the people of Israel out of Egypt so that they could save themselves from slavery, the first prayer made by Moses to God was to help him prove to the people the authenticity of his message. God told Moses to throw his staff on the ground. Hardly had he done that when it turned into a snake. God then told Moses to lift the snake by the tail, and when he did this, it turned into a staff again. By using these miraculous powers Moses was able to win the confidence of his people before uprooting them from their homes.

The Prophet Mohammed was also helped by supernatural powers bestowed on him by God, the display of which

59

established his identity as a messenger of God amongst totally unbelieving and heathen tribes. Mohammad's greatest miracle was to transform those very men into a force which truly reflected the glory of God.

The eigth Sikh guru. Harkrishen Sahib had named his successor in a deliberately ambiguous manner. He said, there is always a hidden purpose in whatever perfect Masters do. The aim was to strengthen the followers' faith in the guru who was so one with God that he hated to expose his presence.

When asked to nominate his successor at his death, he replied, 'Baba Bakale! The news spread like wild fire and reached a village called Bakala in the Punjab, where twenty-two people set themselves up as gurus, each claiming to be his successor. Each one seated himself on a raised and decorated diad and employed public relations men to promote them. The Sikhs were completely confused. If personal propaganda was the criterion, they excelled each other in this. Many had an impressive presence, a long flowing beard, dreamy eyes and a melancholy or smiling appearance depending on the visitor.

Elsewhere, however, a devout Sikh whose name was Makhan Shah was in serious trouble. He was carrying very costly merchandise in a ship which was caught in a storm and was about to sink. Makhan Shah prayed to his Guru to save him and his goods, otherwise, he would be reduced to utter poverty. He had not seen the new guru and the one he had known was dead. But he knew a guru never dies, he is immortal. He therefore promised to donate five hundred gold mohars (a coin like sovereign) if his ship was saved from sinking. His prayers were answered, the storm abated, the ship righted itself and soon made port.

Makhan Shah was immensely grateful to his guru and therefore set out alone to offer the donation he had promised when in distress. On arriving at Bakala, he was told that there were twenty-two contestants to the succession and none knew for sure who was the real one. So it was also his dilemma now. Who should be offered the 500 gold mohars, a very big sum in those days?

He felt that since the guru has to be all-knowing, the true one would know the amount he had promised and would be able to give some positive proof of his identity. He decided to place five gold mohars before each seat and wait to see the results. This he did, respectfully touching their feet with his forehead. Everyone blessed him and showed pleasure in receiving the five gold mohars but none said a word about the incident. Makham Shah was greatly disappointed since he realized they were all fakes. He was determined to find the real once since he could not forget his recent escape which he knew could only have happened through the intervention of his guru.

On further enquiry, he discovered that there was a sadhu called Teg Bahadur, who lived in a nearby cave and refused to come out. He was continuously engaged in meditation and never met anybody except his mother who took him his simple provisions of food and water everyday. Makhan Shah implored the mother to allow him at least to see this sadhu, which she kindly agreed to let him do. On approaching the sadhu, Makhan Shah bowed down and, as usual, placed the five gold mohars, before him. He immediately said, 'Why are you offering five when you promised five hundred?' and laying bare his right shoulder, showed red marks which, he said, he had acquired lifting the ship which was sinking fast. Makhan Shah was thrilled. His tears flowed like rain, tears of joy at having discovered his saviour, his guru. He ran up to the roof-top and, by beating a drum, announced the miraculous discovery of the ninth incarnation of Guru Nanak. Sikh gurus forbid miracles, but there are occasions when they have to resort to them, as on this occasion.

Let us now study the teachings of this great saint, Satya Sai Baba. His word is: 'You are immortal. Awareness of God is your aim.'

> You are the image of God,
> Realize your origin.
> *Guru Granth Sahib*

'You are an instrument of God. Do not attach yourself too much to the part you have been cast to play in the drama on the stage of this world.'

He advocates the shakti path as the easiest and surest way to becoming aware of God and also stresses the need for a satguru who should be devout and totally committed. Similarly, inner purity is a quality demanded of disciples, who must in addition receive God's Grace, without which nothing important can be achieved. Satya Sai Baba's liking for devotional songs and scriptures is well known, and due to this, he is striving to revive people's interest and faith in the Vedus, the Shastras and the Upanishads.

# 12
## Miracles—a Stagnant Path

God's bounties are great. The miraculous powers called ridhi-sidhis are not so difficult to attain for anyone with determination and perseverance. This is the first big stride forward in spiritual evolution, which convinces disciple of the unlimited possibilities that lie dormant in him and which can be aroused by a determined effort under the guidance of an experienced guru. To enter temporarily into a spiritual realm where mundane wishes materialize without the need of mental or physical toil will result in making a wreck of a man.

> Those who will live by toil, and out of this hard-earned fare, give some in charity, they alone can know the path to Salvation.
> *Guru Nanak*

The excitement of being able to perform miracles and being considered a superman by gullible audiences can only be transitory and inconsequential. Yet, it attracts many: witness those who initially set out in search of Truth but end up in a make-believe world of magic. Almost every pilgrim on the path towards God passes through this stage. but only the most powerful souls who cannot be enticed by such transitory gains, rise above them. This high hurdle in the path of spiritual evolution has been put there with a purpose by the Almighty and many simple souls are misled into accepting this illusion as the final goal as the guru cannot take them beyond the stage he himself has reached. Exhibiting these magic powers is frowned upon by Masters of a higher spiritual evolution who prefer privation to miracles. Sita Ram Das Onkarnath once prohibited a great sadhu, gifted with supernatural powers, to provision his empty and poor house for him, preferring instead to fast when he had no food. Christ, who had great spiritual powers, could have easily disappeared, but he chose to die on the Cross as an eternal act of self-sacrifice which anyone could understand. Guru Arjan, whose verses, received by revelation and compiled under the name of Sukhamani, are today recited by men and many faiths to have their desires fulfilled, preferred to suffer torture and death rather than use his miraculous powers.

Miracles by saints and Masters, however, fall into a different category. Often undertaken to relieve the sufferings of deserving souls, they are also done to attract people to God. You will never find exhibitionism in the work of Masters, who are humble and egoless. They attribute everything creditable to God and set a 'down-to-earth' example for all people to follow, though the course they prescribe is not easy and the day-to-day conduct still more exacting. They will tell you that there are no short cuts to perpetual joy. Every step has to be taken by the aspirant himself, who is told bluntly that success depends on the Grace and Mercy of God, even more than on his own efforts. These efforts should be made in accordance with the teachings of the Bagavad Gita, as a part of one's duty, leaving the result in the hands of God.

The reason why all great Masters are known to discourage too much attention being given to miracles is that possession of these powers inflates the ego, thus making further spiritual progress impossible, for which the stress should always be on selflessness and humility. Clairvoyance in particular is granted to people to guide them clearly along the path of spiritual evolution and to build up their faith in their ultimate reality. But if these powers are used for selfish and materialistic purposes, they block the very passages they are intended to open. The disciple is, therefore well advised to disregard any desire to acquire miraculous powers.

# 13

# *Maharishi Mahesh Yogi*

Maharishi Mahesh Yogi received world renown when he received as disciples the Beatles and other celebrated European men and women like Mia Farrow, the actress. The air conditioning plant and other comforts available at his Rishikesh ashram, essentially for the benefit of his European disciples, became a subject of slander, as did the comparatively heavy fees said to be charged at the ashram to affluent followers.

I decided to call on him and see if I could derive some benefit from his experience. I had heard that, according to this Yogi, transcendental meditation is the simplest thing possible. It needs no food or sexual disciples, only the proper technique under his guidance. Even the aim need not be awareness of God; an atheist is welcome to follow his technique. The claim is that you will, in any case, better your worldly prospects by allowing some time daily for transcendental meditation. It appeared an extremely attractive proposition, and I set out to meet the yogi in his ashram on the banks of Ganges at Rishikesh.

After taking a boat across the river I walked up to the ashram which stands on high ground and is surrounded by thick vegetation. On arriving, I found a clean, orderly atmosphere. A beautifully green lawn surrounds the main building, where the Maharishi stays, which has air conditioned underground cellars where European disciples practice the technique of meditation under his care.

I had to wait for some time after being announced, since he was to come out punctually at an announced time, sit on a platform on the lush green lawn and address his European disciples of whom there were about thirty young men and

65

women taking a special course at the ashram. We all stood to greet the Maharishi when he arrived. I bowed as usual and he noticed me since I was in my brigadier's uniform, and smiled with that innocent and charming smile he has, for which I liked him. His English was good and he was logical and extremely pleasant with everyone. The questions I asked him received satisfactory answers. Some other sadhus then appeared, one of whom was clad in white satin which he was self-conscious about, and he appeared keen on attracting the attention of the Europeans to himself. In this group of sadhus was a dark, well-built sadhu wearing only a langoti or a loin-cloth, who was not aware of all his surroundings and appeared to be completely merged in God. I later learnt he was the finest flower in the spiritual garden of Rishikesh. How I wished I could get to know him well, but he never said a word and after some time strolled away like a sweet dream.

Anyhow, the Maharishi asked me to come any Sunday with a length of cloth, and he promised to initiate me into his system of transcendental meditation. However, this was not destined to be, since, when I arrived one Sunday with bed and bedding, the Maharishi was so busy with his European disciples that he asked me through his secretary to come some other day. Since I was keen on learning his technique, I went away rather disappointed.

My next meeting with the Maharishi was along with Baba Sita Ram Das Onkarnath, who expressed a desire to call on him in his ashram. Baba had established his Rishikesh ashram directly opposite the Mahesh Yogi's, and the constant chanting of Nam at Baba's ashram had apparently disturbed the peace at the Maharishi's establishment, and he sent word that the Nam Kirtan should be stopped, since it interferred with his meditation. As Baba had already called on the heads of all other ashrams at Rishikesh, he now decided to call on the Mahesh Yogi as well. Before going there, he sent word to the Yogi and fixed the time of his arrival at the ashram. We were punctual but Baba had to stand and wait a fairly long time before Mahesh Yogi could meet him. Baba did not mind and was all smiles when he met Mahesh Yogi. Baba told the Yogi that the loudspeakers from his own ashram would never in future face the Maharishi's, a solution which appeared to satisfy the Maharishi.

Baba invited Mahesh Yogi to visit his ashram, which he promised to do at 8 p.m. One American disciple, who had left him and is now a follower of Baba, told everyone, including Baba, that Mahesh Yogi would not come before midnight when everyone was asleep so nobody would see him going to another saint. We did not believe him and chided him for speaking ill of a yogi. He said, 'Wait and see.' Baba made me wait at the outer gate of his ashram from 8 p.m. to escort Mahesh Yogi to his room where he had made preparations to receive him. I waited there till after midnight, when Mahesh Yogi's car came, leaving me in the dust at the outer gate. I ran after it and with difficulty caught up with the Yogi just as he was entering Baba's room. Baba embraced him, made him sit next to him on the same platform, clasped hands into his own and smiled his beauteous smile which says 'I love everyone.' 'The guest is the image of God and has to be treated likewise.' It was a lovely scene, where pleasantries were exchanged and I think that Mahesh Yogi went back happy, having seen God in action. I attribute the Maharishi's late arrival to some more pressing engagement, although he never said a word of the reasons for his delay.

I also attended the Maharishi's international meeting at the India International Centre, New Delhi, where I heard his disciples from various countries certify the efficacy of his system. No one spoke in depth, but a great deal of printed matter was distributed at the entrance. Mahesh Yogi spoke well and impressed everyone by his ready wit and charming smile. I saw a rather heavy man sitting in the row immediately behind me almost fly over our heads, to fall flat in the row in front talking incoherently, a phenomenon I have seen before. The man did not appear hurt and was highly animated.

Much has been said in the Press against Mahesh Yogi, a great deal which I consider ill-informed, and encouraged by those who envy his world-wide popularity. In my humble opinion, he has made some useful contribution towards awareness of God in European society whose conditions his method uniquely suits. The mere fact of his attracting so much attention to India is praisworthy. Once their consciences are awakened, people will be in a better position to follow the difficult path of becoming aware of God. Strict disciplines at an early stage would discourage many and the comfort of his ashram appears to be in pursuance of this same principle. We ought to be proud of this remarkable man who has held the attention of the Western world once again following the influence that Vivekananda once exerted in those countries. His philosophy is so simple that it will attract even drug addicts. He excludes self-confidence and lends charm to Rishikesh and India. As time goes on, his transcendental meditation technique may become a subject of study in most universities as the first secular step towards godliness.

One must remember, however, the inherent danger of making the knowledge of acquiring great powers available to evil-minded people who are likely to misuse such powers. That is why there is so much stress in our Shastras on the inner cleanliness and piety of a disciple before the guru initiates him to these limitless powers. Fortunately, there are some in-built checks in our psychology whereby selfish aims automatically lock the entrance to higher sources of power. The damage however, can be considerable even by introducing evil-minded people to lower and lesser avenues of energy and power. And there is a still greater danger of making a man self-centred and unmindful of the needs of society. To develop faith in God, or Truth or Ultimate Reality, or whatever other name you wish to give it, is the imperative need of society. Otherwise, on what grounds should a powerful man take pity on less fortunate human beings? My hope is that the Maharishi will introduce 'Faith' as a vital part of his programme for the second stage of his worldwide campaign.

# 14

## Shri Anandamayi Ma

Behold, now and always one with the Eternal,
I am ever the same.

*Shri Anandamayi Ma*

Having read such glowing tributes to this great woman saint
of Bengal, in the *Autobiography of a Yogi*, I was anxious to
meet her. Surprisingly, just as I was thinking of her at the
Dehra Dun Railway Station, where I had gone to meet a
friend, I saw a crowd before a first-class compartment, and on
enquiring from one of them, I was told that Shri Anandamayi
Ma was going by this train. I pushed my way inside the
compartment where she was seated and, to my
embarrassment, realized that I had nothing to offer to this
great saint, not even the customary flowers. I bowed down to
touch her feet. She sat, graceful and charming, with the smile
for which she is famous. She must have been very pretty when
young. Now in her seventies, she looks beautiful, reflecting a
charm which only people totally one with God possess. A
fleeting desire crossed my mind that she should bless me with
prasad. She understood this unspoken thought and ordered
the attendant to get some fruit from a basket for me. She also
kindly gave me a bunch of flowers she was holding. I
happened to be the only one who was thus blessed by her at
that time. The train soon left, to the accompaniment of shouts
of 'Jois' from her numerous men and women disciples. Her
saintly image had made a deep impression on my mind. I was
to meet her several times after this.

Many miracles are associated with the name of this lady,
one of the greatest and most loving saints, like the fact that on
the very day of her marriage, arranged by her parents against
her will, she was able to convert her young husband, who
became her disciple, and both vowed to lead a saintly life in

pursuit of the awareness of God.

She is one of the finest spiritual flowers in bloom in India and she has a remarkably good influence on a large section of Indian society. A firm believer in the holy scriptures and a follower of Bhakti Yoga, she spreads the fragrance of God's name throughout the land. Being the pride of Indian womenhood and a fountain of spiritual life, many forlorn prople have steadied themselves in the misery of their unfortunate lives through her blessings. May God bless her with many more years of healthy life for the benefit of suffering humanity!

# 15
## Sant Kirpal Singh Ji (1894–1974)

We testify to that which we have seen
and bear witness to that which we know.
*St Paul*

A dying old Parsee lady presented me with a most remarkable book called *The Path of the Masters,* by Dr Julian Johnson, MA, BD, MD, an American baptist Minister who preached the gospel in India as a missionary and came under the spell of a great saint of this time, Baba Sawan Singh (1850–1948) of the Radhaswami sect.

After reading the book, I found that certain awkward inhibitions had been removed and my mind had been cleared of the obstacles implanted there by the study of religion as interpreted by some of the so-called learned men who are so prominent in society. The teachings of the Sikh gurus enshrined in the Guru Granth Sahib assumed a new importance and became an extremely precious inheritance.

When Baba Sawan Singh died in 1948, three exponents of this faith remained still alive: Baba Charan Singh at Beas, Sant Kirpal Singh at Delhi who died in 1974, and the Swami Ji at Dayal Bagh Agra. I learnt that Baba Sawan Singh had great regard for Sant Kirpal Singh who was an engineer by vocation and greatly devoted to the Radhaswami philosophy.

I went to the Sawan ashram at Gur Mandi, Delhi and met Sant Kirpal Singh. He was wearing the simple punjabi dress of silwar and kamiz, and being a Sikh, he also wore a turban.

Sant Kirpal Singh, born in 1894 in Sayyad Kasran, now in Pakistan, was initiated by Baba Sawan Singh Ji, the great saint of Beas, in 1924. While working for the Indian Government and leading the life of a householder, he followed the instructions from his Master for twenty-four years. Upon his

71

Master's death in 1948, he retired to the Himalayas for three months where he lived in seclusion, after which he returned to the world and assumed the role of Guru initiating many thousands of disciples in the practice of Surat Shabd Yoga. He has also written several books such as *The Crown of Life*.

According to Radhaswamis, the soul can only travel along the path of nada or celestial sounds, on its way to becoming aware of God. This nada is termed the 'Audible Life Stream' by Dr Johnson in his book *The Path of the Masters* and consists of musical notes, which fill every conceivable dimension in the form of vibrations, supposedly emanating from and returning to God, which permeate all animate and inanimate creations. Prana, or energy, is only a manifestation of this vibration, as are the different forms of creation which are sustained by this perpetual life stream. This sound can not be heard through the ear, but through the inner organ of hearing, by anyone, after certain disciplines have been observed and a living Master has put one in touch with it. Once the Master has 'switched it on', so to say, it can be heard most distinctly, and grips the attention of its hearer to the exclusion of everything else, causing a natural concentration of the mind on the sourch, which is God. Initially, the sounds, whose variety is endless, are somewhat coarse, like the blowing of a conch-shell, thunder, the ringing of bells, a whistle and such like. As the concentration of the disciple grows the notes become more refined and musical until this exquisite music absorbs the attention of the disciple so completely that he reaches the state of samadhi, the highest possible stage of meditation during which one achieves union with the Absolute.

The Vedanta accepts that the universe was created by this sound called 'Nada Brahma'. It was saute surmad, the sound of the abstract, which Mohammad is said to have heard in the cave of Ghaare Hira. Moses heard this sound on Mount Sinai. Shiva heard anahad nada in the caves of the Himalayas. The New Testament talks of this sound thus, 'In the beginning was the Word, and the word was with God and the word was God.' The Sikh scriptures describe it as 'Panch Shabad Dhun' and by various other names.

It is the astral body, the twin to the physical body, which

has to be activated and attuned to this sound current. Once you ride this current, it only ends in light, the finest vibrations of sound, which is God, an experience achieved by following certain set procedures.

The essential disciplines in this faith are vegetarian food, initiation by a living Master, and constant and prolonged practice as taught by the Master. The company of similarly inclined disciples is also considered desirable for the obvious reason of getting moral support.

On one occasion when I met Sant Kirpal, he explained a passage from the Guru Granth Sahib after which he asked his followers to sit in a nearby tent for the initiation ceremony to which I went. We sat in a special posture, with our eyes closed and our fingers in our ears, for over forty-five minutes repeating the sacred mantra given by Sant Kirpal Singh. I found it tiring, and the presence of scores of others distracting. Sant Kirpal touched our forehead and you repeated the mantra after him. At the end, everyone was asked if he had seen or heard anything. I had seen nothing unusual and had heard only what any ears would hear when plugged with one's fingers, as a result of the friction between the fingers and the outer ear. Many others had done better, and some even announced their having seen visions of some important saints when their eyes were closed. Some had heard what they thought was thunder. It was obvious I was not ready for an instant switch-on. However, Sant Kirpal's personality was pleasant and his technique scientific, though, to my mind, 'Hatha Yoga' in concept.

Here I must confess that whereas during the next two months I continued to do the repetition of mantra japa as taught by Sant Kirpal Singh, I stopped the physical part of plugging my ears and sitting in a special posture, which I associated with Hatha Yoga, and hence was unacceptable to me. One night, after two months, I was woken up at 2 a.m. by loud musical sounds which appeared to be coming from the right side of the head, and the source seemed to be within, or outside my head. I went straight to my prayer room and stayed there for about five hours. The musical note lasted for all this time and ceased as soon as I left the prayer room. This continued unabated for several months. Every morning I would be woken up at 2 a.m. by this sweet nada, which would last during prayer times and then reappear the next morning. This, I attribute to the spiritual powers of Sant Kirpal Singh, to whom I shall ever remain grateful since he gave me the first taste and a positive personal proof of nada. I lost this ability later through my own fault as a result of not observing the disciple of satric ahar, eating only vegetarian food.

## DAYAL BAGH

I met the present Swami Dayal Bagh in Agra, and was pleased to see that the spiritual and economic disciplines, laid down by Sahibji, the previous guru whom I had met as a young boy, were being maintained. The dairy farm at this ashram is very popular and so are the educational and vocational institutions there, which are doing great work for the benefit of humanity. Satsang is regularly held and I am sure many people benefit. The day I went there, the Swami never spoke a word and someone else was deputed to carry out the satsang while the Swami sat in his chair. The whole atmosphere appeared lacklustre to me, and on that day, I think, a tamsic element dominated my constitution and I was unable to appreciate this experience. So I can only blame myself for not enjoying this satsang. The ashram is planned to be economically self-sufficient for the inmates. The small-scale industry and dairy farm have flourished, I hope, not at the expense of the main aim of the pioneers in this line.

## BABA CHARAN SINGH

Marvel not that I say unto you,
Ye must be born again.

I was keen on meeting the announced successor of Baba Sawan Singh, and soon an opportunity offered itself. A large gathering including some Europeans and saffron-clad sadhus awaited the arrival of Baba Charan Singh who was to address them at Beas. I joined this congregation. An immaculately

74

dressed man of middle age with a flowing beard, churidar, silk kurta and a well-tied turban, approached us. Evidently, he was the one we were waiting for. After due salutations, he took his seat on a high pedestal and addressed the gathering, who waited so silently that you could have heard a pin drop. Words poured from his mouth like precious pearls as he spoke of the love of God from the depth of his heart, which had a touching effect and brought tears to many eyes.

I then met him privately in his house, surrounded by well-kept lawns and fruit trees, which he had purchased for himself within the precincts of the Beas ashram. It was indeed a pleasure to be with this man who, though godly, did not appear to be distant. On another occasion, I saw him taking a vegetarian meal at Dehra Dun, where he had come to meet his son. This unassuming common outlook impressed me even more. He never accepts food from any of his disciples, and pays for everything he gets.

On yet another occasion, I was fortunate enough to listen to his talk on the love of God at Delhi where he addressed an enormous, and once again, totally silent gathering. I felt proud to belong to a country which has produced such rare gems of humanity.

There are many men and women of this faith who have made good progress along the spiritual path. Amongst those, however, who become initiated into this wonderful technique are some without a proper cleansing and preparatory period, and, consequently, though the astral body gets activated soon enough by the yoga process, the product does not last. The Radhaswami system is, undoubtedly, a short-cut towards being aware of one's Inner Being, like Yogoda, but you cannot dispense with the initial preparation of cleansing the mind of all impurities like anger, greed, attachment and pride nor with the necessity of cultivating love of God. This preparation is time-consuming and slow but every fruit takes its own time to ripen. Can any crop be raised in an unprepared soil or flourish when the land is full of prolific weeds? Can any unwashed cloth take on a dye? This process appears to lack the stress on Divine Grace, which Guru Nanak and the gurus after him as well as Christ, Muhammad and other prophets

75

considered so important. But I was glad to see Baba Charan Singh stress these qualities, for if the disciple is constantly totalling his own record of yoga practice, of so many hours per day, it must tend to leave him little time to think of the love of God and the need for His Grace which alone can break the bonds and free a man.

The Sikh gurus from Guru Nanak onwards had full knowledge of nada and the jyoti path. They experienced and talked about it daily. Guru Amar Das in particular described it in various hymns which are incorporated in the Guru Granth Sahib. But all of them insisted on the cleansing process through nam sankirtan and nam simran as well as on eradication of the ego by humility and selfless service to the community. The aim is an all-round development of every individual so that while evolving as an individual, he will also be an asset to society, not a self-centred being, concerned only with himself.

In all humility, therefore, I suggest that the Kirtan of Guru Bani be instituted in their congregation halls as a daily routine. Their eminently secular saints would find the finest references for their special technique in the Guru Granth Sahib, the most secular religious book in the world. The hymns in this book are the essence of the truths contained in the Vedas and Shastras, but in a language easily understood by the common man. One cannot think of a Master who does not have a revealed book as his source of authority. I have known Radhaswami saints refer again and again to this sacred book. Let the beautiful hymns of Guru Granth Sahib reverberate as earthly music through their congregation halls and attract the astral music which is the other side of the coin.

# 16

# *Raghubir Singh Ji Bir*

A friend presented me with a copy of *Ardas Shakti,* The Power of Prayer, a Punjabi book by Raghubir Singh Ji Bir, which thrilled me. It expounds beautifully the old philosophy about prayer as preached by Christ.

> For verily I say unto you, that whosoever shall say unto this mountain, be thou cast into the sea, and shall not doubt in his heart but shall believe that these things which he saith shall come to pass, he shall have whatsoever he saith. Therefore I say unto you; whatsoever things ye desire when ye pray, believe that ye receive them and ye shall have them.

I had heard that Raghubir Singh had opened a public coeducational school for boys and girls at Dagshai, in the Simla Hills and was living there. I took the earliest opportunity of going there and found him sitting in his office — a simple man, exuding peace and goodwill. I told him that my only purpose was to meet him and learn something of the Faith from him. He very kindly asked me to stay with him overnight, an invitation which was to give me an opportunity of listening to his translation of a passage from the Guru Granth Sahib, which he did daily during evening prayer.

I enjoyed his kind hospitality and he presented me with some books, a gift I greatly appreciated, as unfortunately, some of his most important works are out of print and not available. I am confident that he is influencing thousands of children, at their most impressionable age, in the best manner possible, since his charm and faith in God cannot but make a lasting impression on the younger generation. This is something which is sadly neglected in modern India under the convenient guise of secularism.

# 17

# *Bhai Sahib Randhir Singh Ji and Other Sikh Saints*

Seek and ye shall find, knock and it
shall be opened to you.
*The Holy Bible*

I was keen to meet this saint who had gone to spend a few
weeks of the summer in the beautiful station of Kunmur Hatti
in the Simla Hills. Therefore, I went to the temple where this
saint was seated. Permeating perpetual joy, this saint spends
most of his time in nam kirtan and listening to quotations
from Guru Granth Sahib. A strict vegetarian who eats only
what is prepared by his daughter's hands and a strict follower
of the Sikh faith, Bhai Sahib Randhir was imprisoned by the
Akali movement who suspected him of being a revolutionary.
He is well-educated and comes from a good family. A friend
had lent me his book *Jail Chitthian,* Letters from Jail, written
during his imprisonment and later developed into a highly
readable book in Gurmukhi script. This book contains an
account of the miracle according to which God himself had
initiated this great saint to the Sikh Path. The incident had
happened in the temple of Singh Sabha, Abbotabad, and as
this was in my own district, it naturally attracted me.

Bhai Sahib, a revered brother which was how he preferred
to be addressed, was quite elderly. He was singing the nam
kirtan to the glory of God, which went on and on, at the top of
his voice. I thought it would finish by 10 a.m. but even at noon
there was no sign of the kirtan ending. When I bowed down to
take leave, he held my arm and would not let me go. Who
could refuse such love and kindness? I therefore stayed on till
the end and later discussed spiritual life with him, during
which time it became evident that he would tolerate no
infringement of the strict path laid down by Guru Gobind

Singh. According to this, there are strict eating restrictions which would make food cooked in the Army messes taboo. I could only follow this path if I left the military service which I was not prepared to do at that stage. I enjoyed his company so much that it was with great difficulty I pulled myself away from him. I later met some of his associates — he does not like to call them disciples — who had benefitted greatly from being initiated by him to the Sikh faith by the ceremony called amrit, the use of sweetened water potencized by recitation of certain prescribed chapters from the Guru Granth Sahib, or pahul.

Guru Gobind Singh has proclaimed the 'Celestial Word' as described in the Guru Granth Sahib as the future Guru of his followers. Previously, he had prescribed initiation by the 'Five Loved Ones', the Piyaras, who sprinkle amrit on the tongue, face and head of the disciple and make him repeat the common mantra after them. It stands to reason that if even one or two amongst these five Piyaras are evolved souls, they sow the spiritual seed as well as a competent guru did in the past, for the combined power of five spiritual men must inevitably be great. Whenever Bhai Sahib Randhir Singh was one of these Piyaras, he would select the other four only if they were really qualified for this high office. The results were instantaneous and often astounding. I heard some remarkable occurrences of men being initiated that were almost flying over the congragation to prostrate themselves before Guru Granth Sahib and achieving a samadhi for days on end. Bhai Sahib also insisted on a long preparatory and cleansing period for aspirants before initiation and was never in a hurry to recruit more people.

I had taken amrit as a young boy and at the time of my marriage, which had the good effect of keeping me permanently attached to the Guru Granth Sahib which today is still the greatest solace I have. But, unfortunately, the circumstances of my military service did not allow me to be initiated by Bhai Sahib Randhir Singh or saints of similar calibre.

I failed to meet two other great Sikh saints: Baba Jawala Singh and Baba Nand Singh, both of whom were known for the great spiritual heights they achieved. I have heard so much about them yet destiny never allowed me to meet them in person. Both were vegetarians and followers of Bhakti Marg, and the miracles they performed were so unusual, even in India, that many Moslems became their devotees, as well as Hindus and Sikhs, the latter though naturally formed the great majority, as Moslems are always enjoined to follow their own Prophet and the tenets of Islam. There are cases on record of Moslems getting sons or having terrible diseases cured after wiping the pages of the Koran with a clean cloth and then drinking water in which this cloth has been rinsed, a procedure prescribed by Baba Nand Singh.

Baba Jawala Singh called Rab, Lord, by Moslems was killed in an accident. He told his disciples about his own death many weeks ahead, and had a wooden coffin made under his own supervision, selecting the site in the river where he wanted his coffin containing his body to be submerged in water, and showing this spot to his close associates, and expired on the due date. His body was physically perfect, he just departed like one going back home after a sojourn in a foreign land. One of his disciples, a brigadier in the army, who could not attend the funeral owing to military duties, did see the whole proceedings in a vision at Madras where he was then posted.

Baba Nand Singh who was a disciple of Sant Karam Singh of Mardan, a frontier province of Pakistan, was so powerful that each one of his disciples found him standing by his side whenever any danger threatened. People came safely through showers of bullets in war and tragic accidents in peace. He ordered that no money should ever be collected for his free kitchen, or for the construction of a temple or other day-to-day expenses. Only construction material or cooked food or stitched clothing could be donated by admirers, and then only strictly as required. Simple villagers would bring cooked food, mostly chapatis, vegetables and dal to the free kitchen where thousands were fed on festive occasions and hundreds daily. Rich men donated bricks, cement, steel or wood, and personally worked as labourers to earn spiritual merit. Those who had no money would volunteer to contribute labour. It was a commune of love. Can there be a better commune? Even now, in Baba Nand's beautiful temple, you are not allowed to offer money in any form, though you can offer flowers or karah prasad, a sweet pudding, which is distributed amongst all present. Baba Nand Singh insisted on reciting gurbani, Sikh sacred hymns, or nam and subscribers' names were listed for reciting such-and-such bani or gur mantra for so many thousand times, as the only fee for the various services rendered by him to his disciples.

His Master, Sant Karam Singh, was a sepoy under the British in the army at Mardan in the Northwest Frontier, now in Pakistan. He was utterly devoted to God and the whole company held him in high esteem. He used to go daily for meditation to a cave on the banks of the river which flowed nearby, for which he followed fixed times for meditation, mostly early dawn and dusk.

One day he was detailed for quarter guard duty which is the pride of any unit. The turnout of soldiers is expected to be of the highest order and their vigilance even more so, since they are guarding all the unit's weapons and ammunition. Weeks of preparation, the starching of uniforms, polishing and cleaning of boots and belts, is not considered adequate, and the guard is mounted only after a thorough last-minute inspection.

Sepoy Karam Singh's duty roster showed him on duty between 7 p.m. and 9 p.m., the hours fixed for his evening meditation. He just could not miss this for the whole world. He left his rifle and bandolier of ammunition at his sentry post and ran off to his cave without thinking of the consequences of deserting his post, for which he was liable to a very heavy punishment. He went to the cave and got so absorbed in his meditations that he regained consciousness of this world only at dawn, which was the time for morning meditation. He completed that also, and returned to the lines at about 9 a.m. next morning. Immediately on arrival he was given the order to report to the Commanding Officer in his office. The seriousness of his crime and his unusual predicament only dawned on him at that time. He vividly recollected having left

81

his rifle and bandolier at his sentry post and leaving his post while on duty, without anyone's permission. It could mean a very long sentence in a civil jail and dismissal with disgrace from the Service. Every soldier knew that. But he was in for a surprise which was to change completely the pattern of his life.

The British CO was looking very cheerful when the Orderly Officer marched Karam Singh in. The CO asked the Orderly Officer to describe the events of the previous night as reported by him in writing. The captain said he had visited the guard at 8 p.m. Sepoy Karam Singh, who was on duty, challenged him to identify himself. The tone of the challenge, the alertness, the smartness and soldierly bearing of the sepoy on duty impressed the captain greatly. Only on shining the light of his torch on the sentry's face he had found that his eyes looked very fierce and red. Suspecting him of having taken liquor, he closely examined Karam Singh but found that his suspicions were wrong. The captain therefore, recommended that he deserved congratulations and promotion. The CO jocularly inquired from Sepoy Karam Singh if he had taken any liquor that night. To this query, he expected no answer because the flawless character of Karam Singh was well known.

Karam Singh now clearly understood that the God to whom he had surrendered so completely had stood as a sentry in his place so that no blame could be attached to his devotee. God must, naturally, have impressed the captain when he saw His face in the torchlight. He was so overcome with emotion that he could not speak a word; tears welled up in his eyes and he made up his mind once and for all to serve the One who had stood by him. Respectfully, he told the whole story to the British officers, and requested to be discharged from the army so that he could whole-heartedly serve God and humanity. Most reluctantly, they agreed.

Sepoy Karam Singh went to live in his favourite cave and became famous among the local pathan tribesmen as a Sikh saint, or faqir. Hundreds visited him, showering all kinds of gifts on him.

Some thieves were tempted to enter the cave to rob and kill the saint. But the moment they entered the cave they became blind, and on realizing what had happened to them, they shrieked for help from the faqir. Baba Karam Singh duly went to their aid and helped them, and then he asked them to take whatever they needed. The thieves refused to do this after the miracle they had personally experienced.

Soon, the local Pathans donated a large piece of land close to the cave upon which a temple was built where Baba Karam Singh used to stay.

Once my maternal grandmother went to receive darshan from Baba Karam Singh and took my mother along, who, on arrival, fell ill with double pneumonia. Baba Karam Singh prescribed a bath in the cool spring close by and eating some radishes. Amazingly, she was instantly cured, which confirmed her faith in him.

Baba Nand Singh carried on the work of his Master Baba Karam Singh with distinction and each one of these saints helped all who came in contact with them to achieve greater awareness of God. The torch was being passed on to deserving successors in the line.

Saints have done the greatest service to humanity, but particularly in the communities in which they were born, by setting a personal example of devotion to God and exhibiting the fruits of this devotion.

# 18

# The 'Word' as the Guru

The Word is the Guru and Guru is the Word. All the
essence is in the Word. If the aspirant obeys the Word, the
Guru will surely redeem him.

*Guru Granth Sahib*

The Bible (JohnI:1) says: 'In the beginning was the Word and
the Word was with God and the Word was God.' God and the
Word are shown as synonimous. Jesus also said, 'I and my
father are one.' Therefore, God, the Word and the prophet or
guru are one. This is also accepted by Sanatan Dharma, or
Hindu ethics.

What is the 'Word'?

Could the ordinary sayings of the guru, or prophets be
considered the Word? The answer is No. Since they may not
have originated from God himself, however much inspired or
true they may be.

Could the hymns, poetry and press contained in sacred
books like the Bible, the Koran, the incomparable Bagavad
Gita, the sacred Vedas, the Guru Granth Sahib, the
Ramayana, the Mahabharata be considered the Word? Before
we answer this question, we have to be sure first whether they
originated from God, which is extremely difficult to answer.
The Gita, though said to be pronounced on the battlefield by
Lord Krishna, was certainly not recorded on the spot. Some
even say that Ved Vyas wrote it himself. Undoubtedly, it is a
flawless philosophy, containing nothing but truth and it has
guided hundreds of thousands along the spiritual path
through the ages. But is it the Word?

The Koran came to the Prophet Mohammad from God, but
was dictated to someone else later. It contains universal truths,
but does it fall into the category of the 'Word'?

84

Shri Anandamayi Ma

Saint Kirpal Singh Ji

Maharishi Mahesh Yogi

Photograph by Dmitri Kasterine
Camera Press London

Baba Charan Singh Ji of Beas

The Dalai Lama

Hazrat Inayat Khan

Shri Baba Sita Ram Das Onkarnath

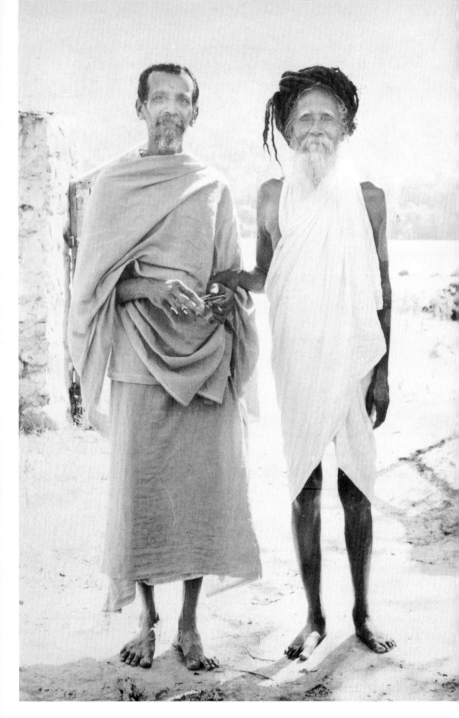

Swami Chidanandaji (left) with Shri Baba Sita Ram Das Onkarnath

The New Testament was written by the Apostles of Christ and has been instrumental in civilizing millions of people. But we cannot say with certainty whether the Apostles meant this sacred book, which they never even saw, to be the Word which was in the beginning.

The Guru Granth Sahib was received direct from Above by the gurus and transcribed by them. In fact, the Fifth Guru, Arjan Sahib, himself compiled the holy Granth, with the recorded word of the previous gurus. The composition, the ecstasy, the theme of Divine attributes and the cosmopolitan nature of the scripture, all contribute to making it authentic. But is it the Word? Can it be substituted for God?

Each sacred book contains some universal truths and some wisdom on the solution to local problems. The prophets were concerned with the day-to-day problems of their disciples and they sought Divine guidance for these, a guidance which was given but was essentially applicable to that race, in that country and under those circumstances.

Universal truths are applicable to all, irrespective of race, time and space, and are the common inheritance of mankind, to be found in every sacred book of all religions.

Besides the Word having to originate from God, it must fulfil another condition, which is, that the whole Universe came out of this Word and is sustained by it. This, obviously, cannot apply to any of the sacred books, though wholly inspired and having tremendous potential for changing the whole psychology of man for the better.

> The vast universe was created through one spoken word (sound). Thus originated myriads of Rivers.
>
> *Guru Granth Sahib*

It is made clear in the Guru Granth Sahib that the Word referred to in Gurbani is a specific sound which originated from God, created the universe and is sustaining it, a fact the Christian Bible also makes perfectly clear. The Koran also verifies this:

> On uttering 'Kun', the universe was created.

The problem now is how to contact this Word which originates from God, represents God as the Holy Ghost, acts as a link between God and the guru of the prophets and later acts, as a guru or guide for the disciple. In the Guru Granth Sahib, the Word has often been referred to as 'Bani' or 'Shabad'.

> This Word is from its origin (God)
> It has removed all my worries.
> *Guru Granth Sahib*

> Five Celestial Sounds are ringing within
> The Lord God has come into my body.

It is clear from the above that these 'sounds', dhunatmik sounds, truly represent God and when one hears them, one is left in no doubt that God has entered the body. How else can God come into contact with a human body? In 'Sthul' or physical form, He is represented by a saint, and in sukshama or astral form, he is represented by 'Celestial Sounds and Light'. The Light has now been proved by scientists to be the finest vibrations of 'Sound'.

There are two keys to this unique spiritual treasure house, which is doubly locked. One key lies in the embodiment of the guru and is the physical key. This is the potencized shabad mantra that a guru gives to the disciple at the time of initiation and is like a 'seed', processed and treated by the guru who has the requisite powers and authority. This seed, once planted in good soil, will bear fruit at the appointed time.

The 'fruit' is the second key which comes in the form of sound and light transmitted by vibrations of varying intensity and establishes the contact with all the astral worlds. Celestial wisdom is then constantly available to guide every action of the disciple who distinctly hears the Command or Hukam, on following which, he can avoid all pitfalls and achieve perfect evolution.

> Obey the Command so that you are accepted:
> Only then you will reach the palace of the Lord.
> *Guru Granth Sahib*

One can only obey if one hears the Command from Above. The hearing of anhad nad, unstruck sound, heralds the capacity to hear this Command directly. At this stage, the physical body of the guru is no longer necessary as he has established himself within the disciple's body as celestial sound, the Word, and though the guru, in his worldly and tangible form, may remain unaware of this, he undoubtedly guides the disciple, wherever he is, from within.

It is self-evident, therefore, that those who put their whole faith into reciting sacred hymns can secure only partial benefits; they may become pious, worthy citizens, beloved by society as men of character but they may still be in a preparatory stage of evolution.

The body is so designed that without the first physical key provided by the guru, there is no chance of coming in contact with the Word, the authentic representative of God in our physical world.

Guru Gobind Singh Sahib, in whom spirituality achieved maximum evolution, gave to his followers a unique gift. He could see no individual capable of guiding his Sikhs, as their spiritual leader. The future as he could foresee it, would demand much more than mere devotion in the spiritual leader. The tyrannical governments of the day, interested in forcible conversions of whole populations, were in no mood to tolerate religious practices which gave so much self-confidence to the slaves, that they challenged the very authority of their foreign masters. The essential truths of Hindu ethos, which also became the principles of the Sikh faith, could only be practised under the protection of the kirpan, the Sikh sword.

Guru Gobind Singh Sahib could find great spiritual saints amongst his followers since the foundation of devotion to God had been well and truly laid by the Ten Gurus, though none of these saints were interested in secular life. He also had great military leaders like Banda Bahadur, who struck terror into the hearts of the Moghals, but did not have the spiritual perfection essential in a guru. Under these circumstances, he devised an inspiring technique in the philosophy of the guru. The whole Sikh Movement was founded on Guru Vad. There cannot be a Sikh without a guru and who could be a better guru than the inspired bani of the gurus, compiled in the shape of the Guru Granth Sahib?

> Accept Guru Granth Sahib as an embodied guru. Those whose minds are pure will discover God in 'Shabad'.
>
> *Guru Gobind Singh Sahib*

Guru Gobind Singh Sahib knew that without the first key no one would be able to find the shabad. The Guru Granth Sahib, which was accepted as the ultimate revelation for the Guru, also advises throughout, the imperative need of getting in touch with saints before any spiritual evolution can take place. Gobind Singh therefore, ordained that Five Perfect Sikhs, the Panch Pyaras or the 'Five Loved Ones', should prepare the amrit or holy water, and, at the time of initiation, deliver this 'key' in the shape of gurmantra the wahe guru or God's nam as uttered by them. They would sprinkle this holy water on the face and head of the initiate and put some in his mouth with their hands.

So the place of the embodiment of the guru was taken by Guru Granth Sahib and the five selected soldier saints, the Pyaras. It was an incomparable device to maintain the devout Sikh community under one banner, believing in truths enunciated by earlier gurus and democratically electing the perfect ones who could initiate all new-comers into the fold. It was a perfect system, elevating the whole community, whereby each and every individual could, by vigorous discipline, attain the position of the Pyaras. The results of such initiation, where conscientious people are selected as Pyaras, have been outstanding. It is a very powerful initiation and my two initiations, one as a boy and the other at the time of my marriage, were beneficial and lasting. In course of time, the seed bears fruit and the initiate is in touch with shabad and God.

The Guru Granth Sahib teaches passionate mystic devotion to God, combined with manly conduct in daily life. Communication with the saints is imperative and is insisted upon, page after page. This scripture contains the very essence of Hindu philosophy bereft of all embellishments and is the supreme example of Indian thought. Its simple diction touches the heart, generating intense love for the guru and God. For those who follow the path of bhakti, I have come across no other religious book which can create the intensity of devotion to an extent that this one does. It further gives proper guidance for identifying the accomplished brahm giani saint mentioned who in turn, gives proof of his perfection and authenticity by constantly referring the disciple back to the bani in the Guru Granth Sahib, as the treasurehouse of spiritual wisdom, which in this age of Kaliyuga, provides those of the Sikh faith with a powerful combination of guidance and inspiration.

There are people who have found God even without being initiated, but simply by having faith in the Guru Granth Sahib as the Guru and by reciting it regularly with great devotion, since it contains nothing but the praise of God and the Guru. Anyone who can acquire faith and develop love for God without the aid of a guru, is possibly already an evolved soul who has been born only to complete the course of evolution. The seed may well have been planted in a previous birth, hence such an individual shows no inclination to surrender himself to any reincarnated soul. Yet even such a person would find it fruitful to follow the advice of the Guru Granth Sahib, and cultivate the society of high souls like saints and siddhas. He may have qualms about adopting anyone of them as a guru, but he certainly can have no objection to the elevating influence of their companionship. A True Saint, referred to as such in the Guru Granth Sahib, will rarely disturb the foundations of faith laid earlier in the disciple. In actual fact, he will strengthen the disciple's faith in his own religion and the path already been followed by him. Anyone who takes you away from your well-recognized path and introduces you to quite a new one is not a genuine saint and should be avoided.

A perfect saint, Guru or Master ought to know all paths leading to God. He will help you in advancing further from the position already attained, and will inspire while he guides, setting an example to be followed. People need someone to inspire them by personal example along their arduous journey, particularly in the earlier stages when the going is very tough. I have seen some high souls universally respected as being evolved, surrendering themselves to yet higher Masters, when they see their own progress has stopped. Some are even sent by their egoless gurus to saints, who they know are the only ones who can give further guidance. Is there any shame in a graduate seeking the assistance of an expert to qualify for his MA or his Doctorate?

# 19

## Swami Muktananda Paramhansa

The yogi who remains content, who has self-discipline and firm
determination and who surrenders his mind and intellect to Me,
that devotee is very dear to me, that devotee is very dear to Me
*Bhagarad Gota*

The 'Sidha Gurus' are the highest in the scale of the Masters,
and to attain this status, both the most meritorious 'Sanskaras'
of the past lives as well as severe austerities and 'Tapasya' in
this life are necessary. It is perhaps the most arduous journey
that a spiritual aspirant can undertake. The aim is spiritual
perfection and there are very few masters who attain these
heights through their own efforts. The path is made much
easier, however, if one is fortunate enough to gain contact
with a Sidha Guru who is kind enough to give the disciple the
initiation to receiving cosmic energy, or Shaktipat Diksha,
which results in an effortless spiritual evolution and the
simultaneous mobilising in his body of all the aspects of Hatha
Yoga. Then he will be able to observe how the Supreme
Goddess Kundalini makes her progress through the various
psychic centres, over which the disciple has absolutely no
control, as it ears away shields surrounding the soul and so sets
it free.

Shri Swami Muktananda was the only other person besides
Baba Onkarnath whom I had heard had attained the status of
Sidha Guru, and on these grounds, I was determined to meet
him. Shri Sai Baba of Shirdi was also known to be a Sidha
Guru but I failed to meet him though I still hope to meet this
remarkable man. Merely the blessing of these perfect Masters
is said to awaken the Kundalini in those deserving their grace.

To practise Sidha Yoga, or Shaktiyat, it is imperative to be
in the are and attention of a Sidha Guru, who alone can
transfer his power of awakening the Kundalini by means of a

word, a Mantra given to the initiate, or by touch, by a glance or by thought transference, which occurs with such power and violence that the grace and guidance of the guru is indisposible.

Sidha Diksha, the initiation by a Sidha Master, demands total surrender, which on the part of the initiate can only come out of intense love, devotion and absolute faith in the Master. There can be no half measures. The Guru is the God embodied. It is His grace which is working through the awakened Kundalini, and all the elements of the physical body are being taken in turn by this all knowing force and are cleansed of the dross accumulated not only during this birth, but in many previous births. The body trembles, sways, adopts the most difficult Yogi Asanas, and dances in superb ecstasy, which under normal circumstances, it would be quite incapable of doing. The body may get heated up and perspire profusely, or experience electric shocks or pains at various points. There may be an involuntary suspension of breathing or such forceful breathing that one may get frightened. The body may get heavy and some part may appear to be dead and cold. There may be a feeling of ants crawling over the body or a snake going up and down the spine. There may be the cracking of bones or a forceful rotation of the body above the waist. There may be unbearable pressures in the heart region and palpitation. One one occasion a companion of mine complained of such heavy pressures within, that she thought she would burst. Constant prayer to her Guru made it possible for her to bear this unusual phenomenon. Eye balls may revolve involuntarily and turn upwards. There may be loss of sleep or appetite. The initiate may start singing or laughing with an uncontrollable laughter. He may experience laziness and death or such increase of energy that he could break down the walls. The body may also become so light that he has a feeling of floating in the air. This physical purification takes innumerable forms depending upon the types of impurities the Goddess Kundalini has to deal with. Some men and women roar like tigers or chirp like birds showing that the sanskaras of their past lives are being cleansed.

Imagine some one in a family undergoing this mysterious

phenomenon and the anxiety it would cause them, particularly when they discover that the best physicians in the town find themselves unable to provide any answer. Even Sri Ramakrishna Paramhansa found himself consumed by some inner fire, whose heat he could not reduce by keeping his body immersed in the cold waters of the river Ganga for hours on end. Fortunately that saintly Lady 'Bhairvi' was close at hand to cure this mysterious malady. And yet there are people who vehemently oppose the need of a Guru in the spiritual field.

A sensitive body, when it is cleansed can also experience phenomena such as visions of Gods and Goddesses, of Saints, of its own Guru in a radiant form, of beautiful scenes, rivers, lakes, springs, flowers and fruits, some of which cannot be described since there is nothing comparable to them in this world. Dazzling lights of indescribable intensity, beauty and coolness are seen and the mind gets rivetted to some balls of light which appear to roll in front of one's open eyes and permeate all animate and inanimate objects. Sounds of flutes, bells, drums, the conch shell or some extraordinary musical notes are heard which keep the mind completely absorbed. Mantras like Guru Guru, Om, Soham, Jai Guru, Wahe Guru, Satnam are heard in exquisite renderings and reverberate through every part of one's body. This is Anhad Nada, the unstruck sound, which emanates from God and concentration on it leads to its Source.

One sees past lives and future events and is able to understand the whole purpose of life. Every event assumes its proper place in the scheme of things; tragedies lose their sting and transitory pleasures their elation. This is how the initiate regains equanimity which is his natural condition. He or she rises above the duality and becomes 'Jivan Mukta' freed from all earthly attachments. A complete transformation of the physical, mental and intellectual status of the aspirant takes place. He now sees himself as a part of his Guru and God, and from now on receives direct guidance from within. There is nothing he or she can do wrong, being completely in the hands of this super intelligence, which regulates all activities of the disciple. Ego and pride disapear as he sees himself as an instrument of the Divine and nothing more. He is now in a position to help others on the path.

The more I read about Swami Muktananda, the more I feel convinced that he is a Sidha Yogi of the highest order. The unusual circumstances of his birth on Vaisakh Purnima, 16 May 1908, alone would indicate a high soul. His mother, a great devotee of Lord Munjunath Mahadeva was given initiation to the mantra 'Om Namah Shivaya', a highly potent mantra from an unknown Sadhu, who appeared out of the blue and before departing predicted the birth of a great seer as her son. The birth took place unannounced in the open, without causing the slightest discomfort to the pious mother, who had come out for a wash in the spacious compound of her house. It was dawn, and the rays of the sun drove out the darkness of the night, bringing the happy tidings of the arrival of one who would illuminate many a soul and liberate thousands from the bondage of birth and death. The boy, appropriately named Krishna, was born intp a rich and pious family on the banks of the river Netravati under a coconut tree. It sounds like a fairy tale but is true. He was a natural leader, behaving as one in his youth. Brave, intelligent and adventurous but not in the normal sense, he was bent upon breaking new ground. The atmosphere created by his religious father in allowing this impressionable boy to see Ramayana and Mahabharata enacted on the stage and to listen to the religious discourses by evolved saints gave the requisite direction to the boy's ambition, that of becoming a Sadhu. What a laudable objective for the off-spring of a rich and pious family.

At the age of fifteen he met his future Master, Swami Nityananda, popularly known as an Avdhoot, a mystic with no fixed abode, who embraced and patted him. This was the signal. He left his comfortable surroundings and ran through the jungle to the monastery of a well known Sidhu named Sidharudha Swami and took Sanyasa, the vow of renunciation. After the death of this Sidha he left Hubli and roamed round meeting many yogis and saints and picking up the gems of their spiritual teachings, that men of his calibre alone can gather.

He was so utterly dependent on God that he asked no one for

food or shelter and used whatever God provided. He spent his nights in grave yards, often using the sheets spread on the tombs to cover his body, replacing them in the early morning. He suffered privations, hunger and disease, practised penances in dense forests and caves until the Kutir at Suki near Yeola attracted him and the vibrations of this sacred place gave him perhaps his first experiences of an awakened Kundalini.

Hari Giri Baba, a sint of great renown, predicted Swami Muktanandi's future by openly declaring him a 'Maharaja' and within two months of this prophesy he met his Master Swami Nityananda again, who had embraced him when he was fifteen. This great Sidha must have been looking for a suitable vehicle which could carry that potent force of Sidha Yoga in its pristine majesty and pass it on to the future generations of seekers of God. It must have been Bhagawan Nityananda's wish to let his successor gain as much experience and knowledge as possible so that he had to give only some final touches to this gem to shine forth.

Bhagawan must have guided him to meet saint Bapumai, a saint who asked only one penny from every one and in the evening threw the collections into the river Chandar Bhaga, saying, 'mother, keep all this money safely for me'. This great saint was to impress on his young mind that Lord Vithal was everywhere. At the age of twenty-two, Swami Muktananda went to another avdhoot, Swami Lingananda at Kashi to learn practical yoga. This avdhoot lived on a burning hot ghat or mountain pass and ate the offerings people made to the dead. He induced Swami Muktananda to stay with him for twenty days and daily see piles of burning corpses. It made a tremendous impact on his young mind but his most unforgettable experience was when Swami Lingananda asked him to feed with his own hands a leper who had blood and pus oozing out of his lips, mouth and eyes and had open ulcers over his whole body. Only with the greatest difficulty could Swami Muktananda persuade himself to put the morsels, with his own hands, into the mouth of this repulsive figure. To crown it all Swami Lingananda insisted that the crumbs that had fallen from the leper's lips into the plate should be eaten by him as prasad. Swami Mukhtananda could eat only one morsel, but Swami Lingananda took the plate from him and with relish ate the rest. At this early stage, Swami Lingananda pointed out the leper's swift and smart gait when he left them and said the leper was none other than Lord Vishwanath Himself. This left an indelible imprint on the mind of the young Swami, that Lord of the universe pervades all and that not much importance should be attached to external appearances.

This reminds me of a similar incident that took place in my home town, Hari Pur. A devotee who was getting his son married, laid on a sumptuous feast to which he invited Sant Attar Sngh who was reputed to be constantly attuned to God. Santji came to the feast, singing bhajans in praise of God as was his custom. He was given the seat of honour in the house and the whole marriage party sang bhajans while the saint was being served food. Meanwhile a wretched looking man in torn clothes appeared at the gate and said he was hungry and should be served first, whereupon he was told by several people that he would be served only after the main guests and that he should not create a row. The noise attracted the attention of the host who came out and after abusing this unwelcome visitor pushed him out. Simultaneously, Sant Attar Singh, who was inside the house, left his food untouched and stood up to leave. Everyone was awe-struck. The host rushed up to the saint with folded hands and asked the reason of his not touching anything on his plate. Santji said 'you have just pushed out Narain himself from your door without food. I am his servant. How can I eat where my master has been shown such disrespect'. The host said he would run after this man, bring him back and feed him in the presence of the Saint. Santji said 'you cannot find him anymore. He came to test your faith and bless you but you failed to recognize him'. The host was adamant; no more than three or four minutes had passed and the beggar could not have gone far. The whole feast came to a stop and many people ran out to trace the beggar and bring him to the feast. But he was never found and Santji went away without eating any of the food.

How often do we fail to recognize the voice of Christ at our door, while going to churches to seek him there!

Returning to Swami Muktananda, we find that he enforced on himself intense spiritual discipline for eight more years at the feet of his Master and attained perfection in Sidha Yoga which he described to his devotees thus:

'There are many pathways to God, generally known as "Yoga Margas". There is, however, a kind of yoga which is above all these and which one achieves by the Guru's blessing alone. The Shastras describe it as Sidha Yoga, because it does not involve practices of Pranayama, Yama, Niyama, the recitation of sacred books, the study of religious texts or even the performance of yajnas. All that is required is the grace of a Sidha Guru, a perfect Master.'

'The speciality of this form of yoga is that while all other yogas involve a certain amount of effort on the part of the aspirant, the process of Sidhi Yoga is automatic. It is therefore also known as Mahayoga, the great path. This yoga cannot be practiced, it begins to happen by the Guru's grace. On reciting this grace, the disciple is immediately capable of practising all other forms of yoga. The functioning of this yoga is extraordinary, and many people find it hard to believe, and this is the main reason why sadhakas and saints do not reveal it to others.'

Talking about his sadhana, Muktanandji described some of his experiences during the nine years of his tapasya before he became a Sidha. They are most informative and are best put in his own words.

'Once Nityanand Baba gave me a fruit and asked me to go to Yeola and continue my sadhana there. I ate it on reaching my destination and sat for meditation. Within moments strange things were happening to me . . . Generally I am a man of great courage, but that day I was overcome by fear. I felt possibly Bhagawan Nityananda was annoyed or displeased with me . . . My entire body started aching, but it automatically assumed Padamasana, the lotus posture. The tongue began to move down the throat and all my sttempts to pull it out failed . . .

My fear grew; I tried to get up, but I could not, as my legs were tightly locked in padamasana. I felt severe pain in the knot, the manipur chakra, below the navel. I tried to shout but could not even articulate. It seemed as if something had stuck, in my throat. Next, I saw ugly and dreadful demon-like figures which I thought were the evil spirits. Strangely, I was fully aware all this time, of what was happening to me. I was consciously witnessing everything.

'I then saw fire blazing up all around me, and felt aht I too was burning. After a while I felt a little better. Suddenly I saw a large ball of light approaching me from the front, and as it approached, its light grew brighter and brighter. It then entered unobstructed through the closed doors of my kutir and merged into my head. My eyes were forcibly closed and I felt as though I was fainting. I was terrified by the enormously dazzling light and it put me out of gear.' . . .

Finally, I saw a blue flame which first grew larger and then diminished to the size of a small pearl. Remaining steady in front of me, it began to sparkle. It was so very beautiful, so enchanting, that I was relieved of all my fear. Now it again grew larger and started going round and round about me.

'All of a sudden my tongue got fixed to the palate hanging in the yoga posture of khechari mudra and my head fell on my chest. I loudly uttered the words "Sri Gurudev" almost unconsciously, and lo! everything became normal from that very moment. All yoga kriyas came to a stop. My hands and feet, which had stiffened, regained mobility.' . . .

'Somehow the morning dawned. I had my bath and a cup of tea, and in keeping with my daily practice, I sat for meditation. Soon I was in deep meditation when funny sounds resembling those of barking dogs or roaring lions, tigers and camels, emanated from my throat. Hearing them, the herds of cattle grazing nearby began to run away in fright. I was sad and dejected, for I had neither heard nor read about this sort of thing happening during sadhana. I thought I had fallen from my path as a result of some curse.' . . .

'I was very conscious of my own self-respect. I disliked begging or pleading helplessly. In the belief that I had strayed from the path of sannyasa, I removed my ochre robes and hung them on a tree, and wearing only a loin-cloth and taking my kamandalu and a shawl in  my hand, I walked away towards the East, leaving the doors of my kutir open, and telling no-one I was going. I thought I might go mad and no one would recognize me.' . . .

'I thus continued walking a long distance and reached Nagad on the third day. There, on the mountain, was an orchard of oranges, sweet lime and sugarcane. I entered it and saw some huts. In a little while, someone from the orchard came running to me and told me that he was Dagdu Singh, the owner. He welcomed me and inquired where I came from and what service I would like to have from him. He owned a big estate and said he was a student of yoga and a lover of sadhus and holy men. He arranged for me to rest in a hut, and ordered khichadi for my meals.

'There was a cupboard in the hut, and as I was sitting there, I heard a voice within me asking me to open the cupboard and read the book lying inside. First I did not pay much attention to it but I heard the same words repeated two or three times. I could not ignore them any longer, so I opened the cupboard and picked up a book. The very page I opened described the yogi experiences I was having. It also explained how a person, who had received shaktipat by the grace of a sidha guru and whose kundalini was thereby awakened, got different kinds of wonderful experiences. After reading a few pages of the book, my mind freed of all troubles and became peaceful.' . . .

## VISION OF LIGHT

'As I progressed in my sadhana, the frightful visions almost disappeared. Yet as soon as I sat for meditation, I would feel I was burning, and at other times, I might see a burning pyre. I used to see a red light and sometimes even different forms and shapes in it. Visions of coming events, of visitors who were to come and of the things they were to bring also appeared, as if in a film. The redness of the light resembled the colour of the horizon at sunrise.'

'Sometimes I used to hear very sweet and melodious divine music. At other times, I would be suddenly inspired to write a poem or sing classical music. I also tasted nectar, a few drops of it dripping in my mouth from the palate. It was a very pleasant experience. . . .

'After some days the red light turned white. It was about the size of a thumb, and would alternately appear and disappear.

'Sometimes I also used to see a golden light which was not always steady. While it flickered, I was at times able to see other worlds in it. I once saw Heaven, swarga-loka. The men and women there resembled us but they were much taller, healthier and more handsome, and they welcomed me. Different types of phenomena or incidents were now visible in the white light, which were previously seen in the red light.

'After the experiences of red and white lights, I saw a black light, about a quarter of an inch in size. It used to appear and disappear, and whenever it appeared, the vision lasted two to three hours during which my mind and consciousness became completely engrossed and calm. A variety of visions, such as those of far-off countries, of movements under sea water, and of great sages and rishis were seen in this light. The vision of each new light added to my happiness. If I saw someone in the black light then that person also was able to see me in a vision or dream, whenever he might be. If anyone came near me, when I was having the vision of black light, that person also would be induced into a meditative mood. The shakti was acting independently in all these phenomena.

'After the visions of black light came a blue light, about the size of a small pearl. It used to come and stand before me but disappeared whenever I tried to look or gaze at it . . .

'Gradually the consciousness of finite self diminished and more and more awareness of 'Being Shiva', Shivoham, 'Being Brahman', aham brahmasmi, began to dawn on me.

'Of course I also had a vision of Vaikuntha, the Abode of Lord Vishnu, and even saw the play of raslila but these were mere visions, not the final reward of sadhana. The ultimate fruit of sadhana or True Enlightenment is obtained when the knot of ignorance is cut.

'Six years passed in this manner.

'The next stage, which takes quite some time after the vision of blue light, is bindhu-bhed or the piercing of the pupil of the eye. It means that the pupils of the two eyes are pierced and in place of normal dual vision, the eyes attain a uniform field of perception. At the time of this bindu-bhed, the eye balls may suffer pains for three to fifteen days just as it hurts during the chakra-bhed, that is, the piercing of the nerve-plexus in the spinal cord. The use of medicine is not advised. The eyeballs start revolving, and in course of time, after many revolutions, both the bindus come together, and when this is achieved, the eyes, though fixed at one point, can see in all directions. This is an uncommon phenomenon and is the secret of what is described as divine vision. After the bindhu-bhed the eyes roll upwards . . .

'Karna-bhed also takes place at the time of bindu-bhed. A chakra, situated at the root of the ear, starts to hurt during karna-bhed. The divine sound one then hears is known as udgitha or Omkar dhwani, and is so very pleasant that I cannot describe it in words. . . .

'After bindu-bhed and karna-bhed, the sadhaka experiences a kind of meditation whereby he sees another separate self of his own. He is puzzled, unable to decide which one of the two is his real self. Such an experience is known as pratik-darshan. At this time his body gets completely purified. Thereupon the sadhaka acquires a feeling that he is merely a witness to everything, and in my case this experience had lasted three months.

'The final attainment comes only when the neel bindu, the blue pearl-like spot of light, remains steady in the vision of the sadhaka. In the beginning it is unsteady. It appears in the vision, sparkles for some time and suddenly disappears, which indicates restlessness of the mind.

## FINAL ENLIGHTENMENT

'As one advances in sadhana, a golden lotus comes, with a peculiar subtle sound of its own, from the sidha-loka and drops on the head of the sadhaka sadhaka who is able to hear the sound as well as feel its touch. It then drops onto the ground from the head, and before he can have a look at it or pick it up, it disappears, an experience I myself have had.

'After this, the neel bindu becomes steady and the sadhaka becomes calm and restful and keeps on looking at the neel bindu. His antarshakti becomes more and more powerful, though his body gets very thin.

'When the neel bindu has become fixed and steady, its lustre always increases and gradually it spreads everywhere, ultimately enveloping the entire universe. The sadhaka now sees in that lustre his Guru or Ishtadeva. He himself then becomes one with his Guru or Ishtadeva, whereby he realizes that God, Guru and he himself are One in essence. This can be termed as real Advaita or non-duality. . . .

No further ways of sadhana remain available for him, he has only to fulfil his remaining fate, prarabdha. Thus, becoming a jivanmukta, he spends the rest of his life for the wellbeing and spiritual uplift of others.'

Guru Nanak talks of 'yan Kand', the Realm of knowledge, in Japuji, the sacred hymns of the Sikhs, while talking of the different realms to which the soul will ascend in its evolutionary flights. He said in 'Gyan Khand' that there are many Sidhas, Buddhas and Naths or Master of Yoga and many Gods and Goddesses. Exquisite nada or celestial music can be heard and infinite joy and bliss is experienced.

Swami Muktananda talks of Sidha loka as the home of the Sidhas, which appears to correspond to the same description as that of 'Gyan Khand'. I found this fact of great interest since it shows the authenticity of people who have similar experiences. Swami Muktananda gives a detaled description of Sidha loka as he talks of the blue bodies of the Sidhas, made of pure consciousness, living amongst trees, flowers and creepers, gardens and mountains, all filled with conscious radiance. They travel on the chariot of thought and keep visiting our world according to their choice.

JAPA YOGA. Swami Mukhtananda goes on to say that there are many Sidhas living here and there in India who do not disclose their identity and it is difficult to recognize them unless they themselves so desire. Swami Mukhtananda lays great stress on Gurubhakti, devotion to the Guru, so that one may earn their grace and achieve fulfilment with ease.

Besides meditation Swami Muktanandji insists on Nama Japa on continuous remembrance of the mantra given to the initiate, which is a highly potent method of spiritual evolution, also known as Mahayajna. Lord Krishna says in the Gita 'of all the yajnas, I am the Japa Yajna'. Guru Nanak says that in Kaliyuga there is nothing better than the singing of the Lord's name and his constant remembrance. Japji is the name of the morning prayer revealed to every Sikh which he must recite daily. In fact Guru Nanak went to the extent of saying

> I live only be reciting thy Name
> If I forget thee I shall die

Japa Yoga is the easiest path and suits all conditions, and, being perfect in itself, it is a means as well as an end. People of all faiths prescribe and practice this but it is a science and there are certain prerequisites to be followed.

God has as many names as he has attributes. Which name will bring the best fruits of Japa Yoga is a question which only a perfect Master can solve. He gives a Name, a Mantra, at the time of initiation which is called a Beej Mantra, or a potencized Sedd Mantra, which is in harmony with the initiate or achieves this harmony by the special powers of the Guru. The constant repetition of this Mantra as 'Nam' brings about the best results, which come quicker if the Guru is a Sidha. Swami Muktananda describes Japa Yoga as Kalpa Viriksha, a wish-fulfilling tree, or Dama Dhenu, a celestial Cow, and Param Chintamani, a gem which yields anything desired.

He also says that 'if the Sadhaka carries out the Mantra Japa after identifying his oneness with the Guru, the Mantra itself and the Lord of the Mantra, then the Mantra instantly activates yoga processes within the initiate, to making him merge with God and become like Lord Shiva'.

Swami Muktananda describes the effect of Japa Yoga on the physical body through the action of the red light; on the 'subtle body' through the white light, about the size of the thumb and located in the throat, on the 'causal body' through the black light which is about half the size of a thumb joint and which lives in the heart; and on the 'grand causal body' through the blue light which is the size of a tiny spot or a lentil which is situated in the navel.

When the tongue, representing the physical body, is satiated through its recitation of the Mantra, Japa enter further and the Mantra begins to be repeated more and more in the throat, representing the Japa of the 'subtle body'. By now the body as a whole, has been purified, and at this stage the disciple has visions of Gurus, Gods, Goddesses, Sidhas and Saints. Then the Japa enters deeper, into the heart. This is also called Shunya or Void, where the Knot of Ignorance can also be found. The speed of Japa increases still further and there is greater joy and enthusiasm. The heat in the head increases and disciple feels warmths throughout his limbs. He can carry out his world activities more efficiently since now inner guidance and vigour is available. He also gets a glimpse of his causal body. Then, suddenly, the Japa moves into the navel. The aspirant feels vibrations in that part and the bluish lustrous body is also perceived. He sees a divine light and all types of states of knowledge, devotion and Yoga are experienced, as all the hidden powers are awakened. Anhad Nada, unstruck heavenly music, is heard and he now gets a Mantra from within by his guru's grace which is the key to consciousness of one's inner Being. At this stage no effort or Japa is involved which continued through the words, heard unconsciously, known also as 'Ajapa Jap'. There is a blissful feeling of oneness with the universe and its creator. He becomes perfect. Nam or Mantra or Shabda is the vehicle which takes one beyond creation to the creator.

You will notice how in a sort of reverse process, the 'Sabda' shakti descends from the tongue, via the throat and the heart to the navel and completes the process in easily assimilable stages. Meditation becomes automatic in this process and no special restrictions are laid down about the place or the time or the duration of the sadhana.

Baba Onkarnath says the same thing and lays great stress on Japa Yoga. In both cases, however, the sadhana becomes easier, because of the Shakti Pat Dikaha by these great Masters.

There are innumerable instances given in 'Shree Gurudev Vanee', the Annual Magazine, of disciples, both western and eastern obtaining similar results. It would take volumes to describe all these variations of spiritual experiences. This Annual Magazine, which contains the personal experiences of some disciples, also has articles by Swami Muktananda and sme of his eminent devotees, which are well worth studying. It clears many a doubt, strengthens wavering minds and acts as a tonic for those on the path.

I think something ought to be said here about the delusion that these Sidhas may cause in the minds of those whom they meet for the first time. I think it is deliberately done to separate the rice from the husk. Swami Muktananda may be found in very rich attire. On occasions he may be made to wear a crown and sit on a magnificently decorated Singhasan or throne. This may put off some disciples who have not yet acquired the vision to look deeper and recognize in him the Sanyasin of three births.

Sai Baba of Shirdi wore a torn shirt but his incarnation the Satya Sai Baba wears rich attire and lives and travels in the conditions of comfort which modern civilization provides.

Raja Janak may have disappointed some disciples with his style of living but he was the greatest renunciate known to history.

One should see the ease with which such men sit on the bare floor or live on just nothing. Often they accept such garments and fineries to please their most devoted disciples and discard them or give them away as if it was trash. That is the sign of a true Yogi or renunciate. I have seen some remarkable saints in silk robes and some others in self-imposed poverty. Let us pray to God to give us wisdom to respect the Divine in whatever shape it appears before us.

I have not yet had the privilege to have the darshan of this great saint of today and have written this chapter as a humble offering at the feet of a renowned Master, with the prayer that he, in his kindness, may make it possible for me to touch his holy feet.

# 20

# *The Dalai Lama*

By Faith you shall be free and
go beyond the realm of death
*Suttanipata*

The role of Guru in its most exalted form was practised in
Tibet where the 'guru', the Dalai Lama, was not only the
Avalokiteshwar Avatar of the Buddha, but was also the ruling
monarch, with unrestricted powers, which the status of God-
King alone bestowed. The mere mention of the words Tibet
and Dalai Lama conjure up vision of unparalleled peace, seclusion and purity in the minds of spiritually inclined people
throughout the world. The mountain Kailash, the abode of
Lord Shiva, and Mansarovar, that beautiful and vast lake at
its foot, were places of pilgrimage for devout Hindus. The
'Forbidden Land's' capital, Lhasa, with its picturesque Potala
Palace, was the goal of life for many an adventurer. This was
the land which converted great Mongol conquerors into
faithful disciples of the Dalai Lama. Even the British Commander, Sir Francis Younghusband, who went to conquer
this rosary-wielding nation could not remain unaffected and
describes how his mind was illuminated by spiritual light,
which proved to him the utter futility of his venture.

Tibet appears to be so positioned geographically as to form
a natural sanctuary for spiritual aspirants from the lustful,
material world. Its vast and mostly uninhabited high plateau,
known as the roof of the world, produces just enough to feed
its small population. Huge mountain ranges make it almost
inaccessible. There is little of importance which would attract
greedy nations to conquer it, apart from its strategic importance and its vast emptiness. All these circumstances
combine to make this place into a spiritual heaven for the
whole world. That is why almost every Tibetan house produces

lamas or gurus, and almost every man uses a rosary of some sort.

Formerly, the monasteries were very powerful institutions, and centuries of peace and the Buddhist faith had left a marked imprint on the hardy population. The Dalai Lama was traditionally discovered by a spiritual process at a very early age and then trained intensively for the role he had to play, during which the greatest stress was on the tenents of Buddhism, which was the state religion.

His Holiness, the Fourteenth Dalai Lama of Tibet was discovered, in the Amdo area at the age of three and gave remarkable proofs of his excellent brain power as well as his spiritual evolution. When the Thirteenth Dalai Lama died in 1933, called the Year of the Water Bird in Tibet, the search to locate his reincarnation began. It is believed that Dalai Lamas who remain celibate, reincarnate themselves for the benefit of humanity. They are all reincarnations of Chenrese, the Buddha of Mercy. The search for the fourteenth Dalai Lama began according to the old custom, by consulting the oracles and learned lamas.

Curious cloud formations northeast of Lhasa were one sign pointing towards the birthplace of the incarnation. Then the dead body of the thirteenth Dalai Lama, which had been placed on the throne facing South, had in a few days changed its position and the face had turned towards the East, another indication of the direction in which to look.

The Regent, a renowned lama, then went to the sacred lake of Lhamoi Latso of Chokhargyal, about ninety miles south-east of Lhasa. In this lake, pious lamas can see visions of the future, which take the shape of letters as well as pictures of events and places. After several days of prayers, the Regent saw the vision of letters Ah, Ka, Ma, followed by a picture of a monastery with jade-green roofs and a house with turquoise tiles. A party of lamas went to Kumbum Monastery in the Amdo area and recognized the roofs of the vision. They also recognized the turquoise tiles on the roof of a farmer's house in the village of Taktser close by and learnt that the farmer had a two year old son. The real leader of the party, lama Kewtsang Rimpoche of the Sera Monastery, dressed as a servant and went to the servants' quarters of the farmer's house while a junior official, disguised in good clothes, posed as the leader. The infant boy went straight to the real leader, told him his correct name and removed from around his neck the rosary which had belonged to the thirteenth Dalai Lama. He further identified and named the other members of the party also.

More tests were carried out in which two identical black rosaries were offered to the boy who unhesitatingly picked up the one belonging to the thirteenth Dalai Lama. The boy also recognized the drum and the stick used by his predecessor. It was later learnt that the thirteenth Dalai Lama had halted in this area and appreciated this farmer's house, saying it was beautiful.

When the incarnation was discovered, the Chinese Governor who controlled that area at that time, demanded one hundred thousand Chinese Dollars as the price for allowing this boy to go to Lhasa. After this sum was paid, he became more greedy and demanded another three hundred thousand, which was also paid. But it meant two years of negotiations before the boy was allowed to leave for Lhasa. A journey lasting three months and thirteen days then followed. At the age of four-and-a-half years this boy was seated on the lion throne and proclaimed the fourteenth Dalai Lama, the reincarnation of Buddha of Mercy. At the age of fifteen, he had to contend against the Chinese military occupation of his country and in 1959, at the age of twenty-four, he had to escape to India, his spiritual home.

Here is the telegram Mr Nehru sent to HH the Dalai Lama as he crossed into India after his escape from Tibet.

'My colleagues and I welcome you and send greetings on your safe arrival in India. We shall be happy to afford the necessary facilities for you, your family, and entourage to reside in India. The people of India, who hold you in great veneration will no doubt accord their traditional respect to your personage. Kind regards to you.'

The Chinese military occupation of Tibet, which according to them, is their 'autonomous' province, was tragic, to say the least. It was like a great steamroller levelling small hamlets in the vicinity of a palace, with no other aim but uniformity of surroundings as a proof of power of the ruler. Tibet had lost its autonomy, but the Chinese lost their moral sense and spiritual men the only possible sanctuary in this materialistic world.

There was a thrill of joy in millions of hearts when they learnt of the safe arrival of the Dalai Lama in India. To my mind the 'precious jewel' was saved by God's own hands so that he can fulfil the purpose for which he has volunteered to re-incarnate.

Tibet and its colourful spiritual history have interested me since childhood. I have read all the books on this subject I could lay my hands on, and have dreamt that some day I would visit the country. It could only have been a dream, since Lhasa, the capital city was forbidden to foreigners even in the time of the Dalai Lama. Now with the Chinese occupation, nobody can even get news about it, much less visit it.

Imagine my surprise and delight, therefore, when I learnt about the arrival in India of His Holiness in person. I soon found an opportunity to meet him in Mussoorie, and sought a private audience which was graciously granted, even at short notice. His Holiness was scheduled to visit the Tibetan School that evening when I reached Mussoorie, a hill station in India, unannounced. First, there were certain security and other formalities before I could be admitted to the waiting room. His Holiness's sister, alas, since deceased, who managed the house, asked me to wait till His Holiness returned from an engagement. I waited till about 11 p.m. when he came back. I had not had any dinner nor made any arrangements for it. But the Dalai Lama very kindly enquired about my dinner and was surprised to know that I was a vegetarian. Soon he ordered some dishes and made me eat in his presence, while he got busy with his spiritual lessons which his tutor had prescribed and had to be done before going to bed.

> That monk of wisdom here, devoid of desire and passion, attains to deathlessness, peace, the unchanging state of Nirvana.
>
> *Suttanipata*

I looked at this beautiful face again and again. It exuded peace and was continuously smiling. He laughed at even small matters and the laughter was bewitchingly honest and from the heart. I felt every word he spoke came from his soul, for it was a soul, a very high soul who was speaking to me. His presence held my attention and added perspective to the holy talk. The Dalai Lama said he was a Buddhist lama and did not believe in violence; His life's duty was to preach non-violence and good will towards all, including those who had forced him out of his country. Naturally, he loved his people and his country, concern for their welfare was his dominant thought. He gave me the impression of a heavenly body which had descended on this earth, which was ill-prepared to receive it. A flower in a desert, but what spiritual fragrance! What peace in such enormous tragedy, and that charming smile which said, 'I understand everything. These are children's pranks. They will understand in course of time and all will be well.' He held nothing against Mao Tse-Tung or other Chinese leaders but offered prayers for their deliverance from ignorance. He of course had intense love for India, his spiritual home, and for Jawaharal Nehru, then our Prime Minister. I felt at that time his adoration of Nehru was almost as great as mine. As a true embodiment of Indian culture and moral principles, Nehru had given asylum to this great spiritual leader and his followers without worrying about the Chinese enmity that this act was bound to generate.

This was one of the proudest moments of Indian history, which was repeated on a still greater scale by Nehru's daughter, Mrs Indira Gandhi, by first giving refuge to millions of Bangla Deshis, Moslems, during the Bangla Desh war of 1971.

I took several other opportunities of meeting the Dalai Lama for whom I began to feel great love, an affection I found reciprocated. I visited him with my whole family at Dharamsala, a Himalayan hill station where His Holiness has built his lodge. I found in him consistency and love for all, but specially for those in unfortunate circumstances like his own countrymen. He is enlightened and has proclaimed widely that if his people do not wish to be ruled by him, he will willingly forego that privilege of service to his nation, in view of the fact that all he wants and prays for is spiritual evolution in complete freedom for the Tibetan people. I am convinced that his spiritual power will create the circumstances for this to happen and, perhaps, without having to resort to violence, his nation will achieve their goal.

The most important meeting that I witnessed was between him and my Spiritual Master, Baba Sita Ram Das Onkarnath. Both were keen to meet each other and when they met, it appeared as if two avatars, one of Vishnu and one of Buddha, were meeting, coming from the great brotherhood of saints. Both parted full of love and respect for each other, a sight for the gods to see. What actually transpired is too vast a subject to be dealt with here, though I hope to write about it later in a separate book. Suffice to say here that Baba started daily prayers for the well-being of Tibet, which were repeated in all his ashrams throughout the length and breadth of India, and Baba's undertaking itself was the guarantee of its success. His Holiness, the Dalai Lama was requested by his high officials not to go to meet Baba because of his own status of incarnation and King. But he ignored their advice and said 'Baba is the older man and a great sadhu. It is my duty to go to him.' This was the true test of an incarnation and the spiritual greatness of the Dalai Lama.

## BUDDHA'S INCARNATION SPEAKS

On an earlier visit to Delhi on Buddha Jayanti, on an invitation of the mahabodhi Society and the Government of India, His Holiness, the Dalai Lama was greatly moved when he visited Rajghat, where Mahatma Gandhi was murdered, and he says in his book *My Land and My People*: 'I felt I was in the presence of a noble soul, the soul of a man who, in his life, was perhaps the greatest of our age, the man who had continued till death itself to preserve the spirit of India and mankind — a true disciple of Lord Buddha and a true believer in peace and harmony among all men . . . standing there I felt I had come in close touch with him, and I felt his advice would always be that I should follow the path of peace. I had and still have an unshaken faith in the doctrine of non-violence which he preached and practised. Now I made up my mind more firmly to follow his lead whatever difficulties might confront me. I determined more strongly than ever that I could never associate myself with acts of violence.'

Elsewhere in his book he says: 'I have absolutely no hatred in my heart of the Chinese people. I believe it is one of the curses and dangers of the present age to blame nations for the crimes of individuals. I have known many admirable Chinese. I suspect there is nobody in the world more charming and civilized than the best of the Chinese . . . Most Chinese would be bitterly ashamed if they knew of these deeds. We should not seek revenge on those who have committed crimes against us, or reply to their crimes with other crimes. We should reflect that by the law of Karma, they are in danger of lowly and miserable lives to come and that our duty to them, as to every being, is to help them to rise towards nirvana.'

This Spiritual Prince of Dharma lives now at Dharamsala, a hill station in the Himalayas. For the first time, the name of this place makes sense. Hundreds of lamas come to this holy of holies and chant mantras in beautiful rhythm till the Himalayan ranges pick up the strain and carry it across the Indo-Tibetan border to the men and women within Tibet who have not heard this sound for fourteen long years. The spiritual vibrations of so many devoted souls under the guidance of the incarnation is a most powerful force on the side of peace and universal love. Perhaps, this Prince of Peace will be instrumental in cementing the bonds of friendship between two of the most populous nations of the world which were torn asunder in indecent haste. No incarnation has stayed in the wilderness after fourteen years. The night is almost over and, although it looks darkest before dawn, the very intensity of the darkness is the sign that the Sun is about to rise. Only spiritual giants like Christ are called upon to suffer and their suffering has never been in vain.


## TIBETAN RELIGION

Essentially, it is the Buddhism of Mahayana, the Greater Vehicle, that Tibetans follow. Mahayana Buddhism aims at the highest stage of nirvana not only for one's self but all others inhabiting this world. This is a doctrinal path, the Gyan Marg

111

while the Tantric element, which is a later introduction of Mahayana is studied separately after the main part has been thoroughly imbibed. Being a profound study, it needs an extensive development of the mental intellect and faculties. In the earlier stages, the sacred scriptures are learnt by heart, followed by discussions amongst the gurus and their disciples and ultimately concentration and meditation are practised to train the mind for the higher study and practice of this intellectual, rather than emotional, religion. There are thousands of volumes in its literature which would need a lifetime of study and are extremely difficult to comprehend.

His Holiness, the Dalai Lama is an incarnation of Lord Buddha, and has taken birth not under the law of Karma which applies to all those who have not yet achieved nirvana but because of the innate desire of Buddhas to be re-born in order to help others achieve nirvana under their guidance and training.

Lord Gautama Buddha Siddhartha was born about 650 BC—about the same time as Confucius was teaching about ethics in China, when Zarathustra was the popular saint of Persia and Lao-Tse was carrying out reform of the religion of China. All these religions believed in non-attachment, vairag; non-assertion of the self, called Wu-Wei by the Chinese sages, and the doctrine of karma, called Yin Quo in Chinese. China's misfortune has been that it has not produced a great living Master for many centuries, while Buddhist philosophy in Tibet produced some iritual personalities. The present Dalai Lama is a product of the same mould. Tibetan Buddhists believe that during the present kalpa or age, a thousand incarnations of Supreme, and perfect Buddhas will come into this world. They further believe that each of these Buddha incarnations will preach his own doctrine and will work eternally for the salvation of all mankind. Lord Gautama Buddha was one of those thousand Buddhas. Original in Tibetan Buddhism is the introduction of tantras, training in the method of spiritual evolution, in addition ot the earlier teaching of sutras, doctrinal treatises.

What a wonderfully liberal idea is that of the thousand in-carnations of Buddha, each with his own doctrine, applicable

112

to and beneficial for the stage of development of his followers. Essential spiritual truths are immutable, but techniques and methods must vary according to the material the Master, or Buddha, has to deal with. The Buddha himself preached three sermons after attaining Enlightenment. The first one, at Sarnath near Benares, was meant for people with limited spiritual outlooks and to them he preached the Four Noble Truths. The Buddha said, 'This is true suffering: this is true cause; this is true cessation; this is the true path.' The true cause of all true suffering was karma and delusion. True cessation was the disappearance of these sufferings and their causes. The true path was the method advocated so that true cessation could be achieved.

The second sermon was delivered at Girdhakuta, in which he talked of Shunyata or voidness. The audience was composed of Mahayanists of the highest intellect. Such a deep sermon could only be comprehended by the elite amongst spiritualists.

The third sermon at Vaishali was delivered for the benefit of Mahayanists of lesser intellect.

The essential nature of Samsara is misery, which is the other name for delusion. It is this delusion of the individual undisciplined mind which is responsible for bondage and re-birth. If by some method the mind, which is intrinsically pure, can be disciplined, the delusion will disappear, thereby exposing the soul to the Truth and achievement of liberation or nirvana. The mind is vitiated by the flow of evil thoughts which has to be stopped as an essential part of spiritual discipline before soaking it into the divine dye. The method is logical.

Firstly, hold back new dirt, or evil thoughts from further soiling the already dirty linen, or the mind, which has become black with dirt accumulated in several earlier birth cycles.

Secondly, cleanse the earlier dirt by thorough washing in Dharma:

> This Mind has become jet-black with dirt accumulated through several births.
>
> *Guru Granth Sahib*

113

Dharma, called chos in Tibetan, means 'to hold back from impending disaster', and all means to achieve this end constitute religion. These means essentially consist of all righteous activities of mind, body and speech, mind being the main component since it originates all action and inaction.

The flow of evil thoughts is stopped and the cleansing noble thoughts inserted, by resting the restive mind in concentration, on one's own physical body or mind or on external objects of contemplation like images. The tantric images for contemplation have been most thoughtfully designed to suit the physical, mental and sensual aptitudes of different individuals. There is also considerable emphasis on the correct pronunciation and recitation of mantras. A guru or lama is absolutely essential to guide the disciple along this path.

In the whole of Buddhist religious philosophy, the emphasis is on the reconditioning of the mind as will be clear from the following story, taken verbatim from His Holiness, the Dalai Lama's *My Land and My People*.

'Once long ago there was a famous lama whose name was Drom. One day he saw a man walking around a stupa. "Look", he said, "it is quite a good thing that you walk around a stupa. But it would be better to practice religion."

"Well, I had better read a holy book then," the man said to himself. And so he started laboriously reading from a book till one day Drom happened to see him again.

"Reading from a holy book is no doubt very good," Drom said, "but it would be better still if you would practice religion."

And the man thought: "Even recitation is no good. How about meditation?"

Before long, Drom saw him in meditation and said: "It is no doubt very good to meditate. But it would really be better if you would practice religion."

"Pray, what then do you mean by practicing religion?" the bewildered man replied.

"Turn your mind away from the forms of this worldly life," Drom told him. "Turn your mind towards religion." '

# 21

## Shri Baba Sita Ram Das Onkarnath

To restore Dharma I shall be born from age to age
*Bhagavad Gita*

### I

My meeting with this prince amongst the loving saints of India took place under miraculous circumstances. My mind greatly urged me towards a spiritual life, and I had read several inspiring books and met a few saints, but my mind still craved for someone who could generate true love for himself in my heart, for it is only mutual love which can weld a disciple and his Master into an inseparable union of hearts, and act as a stimulus to spiritual advancement. Faith, knowledge and such other things are of secondary importance.

I accidentally met a Bangali lieutenant-colonel about twenty years after our first meeting when we were both very young hopefuls at the military academy at Peshawar. At our first meeting we had instantly become friends, but had later lost contact with each other. Then, when I was posted at Mhow, I found that this boyhood friend was our next door neighbour. He was now deep in the spiritual world. He mentioned that a well-known Bengali saint, Baba Shri Sita Ram was observing Mauna, a vow of silence, at Onkareshwar, an island in the river Narbada, some forty miles away from Mhow. I suggested that we should, at least, have immediate 'darshan'.

On reaching Onkareshwar, we found that Baba was in mauna for an indefinite period; he did not meet even his disciples who had surrounded his underground cell with straw matting and he came out only to collect his sparse and tasteless meals. However, at such times, the main disciple sometimes

115

exchanged written notes with him on important matters. On the morning of our visit a disciple called Govind Ji was going to Ujjain and had sought permission for parnan, or obeisance, through a written note, which was not granted. He told us there was no chance of us seeing Baba on that day.

However, on our insistence, he wrote a note to tell Baba that two army officers awaited his kind permission, for darshan and, after leaving the note in front of the closed door of the meditation room, he tip-toed back out of the matting enclosure, apprehensive lest Baba be annoyed with him. We waited outside, occasionally glancing through holes we had made with our fingers in the straw matting to see the fate of our note. After some time the door opened. Baba came out, saw the note under a pebble in front of his door and took it inside. He soon returned and, replacing it under the pebble, turned his back and stood aside. We alerted Govind Ji: he hurried inside, retrieved the note and, reading it, his whole face lit up. Baba had replied: 'They can see me and do parnam from a distance. You can also do the same. I will go back in after a couple of minutes.' We almost ran in and after one glance lay down prostrate in the hot dust that surrounded his room on this mid-summer day. We got up and he went in. That was all. We were very happy and thanked Baba for his kindness, and Govind Ji promised to let us know by telegram the day Baba broke his silence so that we could meet him.

During this brief darshan I noticed that Baba looked intently into the eyes of my companion and it appeared as though he had passed something, through his powerful stare, to my companion while Baba's glance at me was cursory. I mentioned this fact to my companion who had perceived nothing unusual.

On our way back, we went to meet a nanga or naked sadhu in the jungle at Onkareshwar about whom we had heard a great deal. This sadhu talked to the flowers he tended on behalf of Mother Narbada, the Spirit of the River, and spent all his time in this manner. Villagers brought him food and feared him for his miraculous powers. On our arrival, he came out of his flower bushes and, laughing innocently, he said, 'Have you been to the great one?' We nodded our heads in confirmation. How did he know all about our movements? After making us sit down on a gunny bag clcse to the fire which he kept burning day and night, he took a conch shell and started blowing it. My companion trembled, caught hold of my hands and said, 'Request the sadhu to stop making this sound.' He was trembling all over and clutching me with all his strength. When the sadhu stopped blowing, my companion recovered but said something had happened to him and that the earth appeared to have left from under his feet.

That night when my companion sat for his meditation, he saw a vision of himself being transported by a strange zooming sound, on both sides of his body, which carried with it his tiny self sheathed in light. He got terribly frightened, forced his eyes open and walked out of his room. His second attempt produced the same results. He woke up his wife, asked for some tea and went peacefully to sleep. When he told me all this the next morning, I told him that Baba had clearly 'poured' something into him, finding his body receptive. He replied that he had not undergone any initiation from a guru and as, therefore, afraid that he might happen. Baba was to endorse this experience later at the time of my companion's initiation.

One day, I had an overwhelming urge to go to Onkareshwar and see Baba. The monsoon had just finished, and the ferry over the Narbada River had not yet resumed regular crossings. Everyone advised against my going that day. However, the temptation was too strong to resist. On arriving at the ferry, the boatmen agreed to try their first crossing with me on board. The water was turbulent, but it only seemed to help us cross faster. On reaching the ashram I found that Baba had broken his silence on that very day. The disciples were amazed to find us there that very moment.

I met Baba and was delighted with the opportunity. He appeared to know all about Sikh religion. He had been associated with some highly evolved followers of Baba Siri Chand, the famous son of Guru Nanak, and he recited Japuji and Sukhmani and had studied the Guru Granth Sahib. I explained to him my natural love for my own religion, and he was kind enough to take me under his wing to guide me along

117

the path I had followed since childhood.

In Baba I saw my own father who had died after an exemplary life of virtue. But Baba's love was greater by far; I had never come across such disinterested love anywhere else, even amongst the great sadhus I had met. Baba was love personified, and I soon became very relaxed with him though intensely respectful. I had found a fathomless treasure and I was determined not to part with it at any cost.

In his ashram the main emphasis is on the recitation of the maha mantra or the Lord's nam. At all hours of the day and the night, the sweet melody of the nam kirtan could be heard in Baba's ashram. I was to find out later that this was Baba's trade mark.

> I am a dealer in nam
> Nam is my total stock in trade
> *Guru Nanak*

Talks by Baba are rare but whenever he talks, the stress is on nam. He would sleep, if consistent consciousness of God can be so termed, on the bare floor where nam was being sung, unconscious of the bodily discomfort. He would wake up the moment people doing nam kirtan dozed off at night.

> I live only when I recite your name
> I die when I forget you.
> *Guru Nanak*

Next to nam, the stress is on dharma. He insists on strict adherence to the holy scriptures, the revealed Vedas and Shastras, and no deviation is permitted. Pure, something more than vegetarian diet is prescribed and ancient disciplines are enforced. He knows they are difficult to follow, but to achieve something worthwhile the effort has to be proportionate. He is strictest with Brahmins and very rightly so since they are supposed to be the spiritual leaders and any flaws in them would be repeated by their numerous followers. The structure of society in India had been intended to promote spiritual evolution; society therefore was divided into various castes and to each of the castes certain duties or dharma, were assigned in accordance with the nature and the quality of the blood of the people of the caste. When duties are well-defined, they are not difficult to follow. However, now that the accent of the modern world is on improving material life, which necessarily is accompanied by considerable mixing of the castes, dharma becomes difficult to define, and tantric methods of spiritual advancement, which are universally applicable, have to be resorted to. Hence, the stress by all present-day saints is on the recitation of nam, which is equally efficacious to all castes.

In order to prepare the body as a proper vehicle for the descent of the Nam, the Holy Ghost, certain disciplines are considered essential by all great saints for a spiritual aspirant: pure food, social contacts mostly with those who are devoutly religious, patience, continence, austere practices and selfless love, qualities Baba stresses by his own personal example. I have not come across anyone who lives, or even can live, in as 'God-saturated' a fashion as Baba has lived from his childhood. His impact is immediate on all those who come in contact with him, provided their system is prepared to receive a powerful dose of his influence.

To the common eye, Baba looks old and very thin; his hair has become matted through years of tapasya. When the Dalai Lama asked him the reason for his matted hair, he said 'neglect of body care, and not design'. He is so busy with God that he has no time for anything else. He is scantily clothed and always barefoot. Always smiling, he is happiest under, seemingly, the most difficult circumstances. Rich and poor receive equal treatment — though needy ones always get pref- erence. His conversation is always sweet and interesting. He personally attends to all his correspondence, which is never allowed to accumulate. All money is spent either on pro- pagating the Lord's nam or feeding and otherwise fulfilling the needs of the poor. Even those who cannot get their daughters married owing to financial hardship can leave the responsibility on his shoulders and it will be discharged to per- fection.

Love, nam and dharma disciplines attract only those who are no longer in the firm grip of the material attractions of the Kaliyuga. When people talk of gurus today, the speak mainly about the miraculous powers mostly affecting material well- being. There are miracles of the body and those of the spirit.

Thousands of miracles, of both kinds, are attributed about Baba by those who were affected by them. Baba characteristically disclaims any hand in them and says he is completely unaware of these things. In his kindness, however, and to confirm my faith, he made me a witness, almost daily, of unbelievable events.

I have known him make people conscious of their present, past and future, by a mere touch of his hand on their forehead. I have been in close contact with one such person who had no special powers before coming in contact with Baba and one day, Baba specially blessed this person in my presence. Since then, we have prior knowledge of every major event concerning us. Before the Chinese withdrew unexpectedly after invading India in 1962, this person clearly saw Baba in a vision raising his hand towards them and saying 'Stop and go back' and only a few days later, the country learnt of the Chinese withdrawal.

Many see visions after practising austerities but how many can transfer this power to ordinary people by the mere touch of a hand?

The late Pandit Nehru, who was loved by my whole family, was seen at the exact time of his death, being carried heavenwards in great honour, in the lap of Lord Krishna. I was many hundred miles away from Delhi and was foolish enough to ring up the Sub-Area Commander to inquire if he could confirm the 'rumour' of Pandit Nehru's death. He censored me for saying something no responsible officer should say without confirmation. But this same officer later rang me up to confirm the news, at the same time expressing amazement as to how it could have travelled unofficially so fast to the remote place where I lived. After this vision I never entertained any doubts of the spiritual eminence of Pandit Nehru, though people talked of his agnostic attitude of mind. The proof was crystal clear.

Blessed are the pure in heart for they shall see God.
*Lord Jesus*

I have positive proof of Baba's spiritual part in the liberation of Bangla Desh and the release of Sheikh Rahman

120

Mujib. A close relative of Sheikh Mujib who met Baba in Calcutta, is a witness to this unbelievable miracle. In the morning, Baba prayed for Sheikh Mujib's immediate release, and in the evening, Mr Bhutto announced on the radio his intention to release him unconditionally. There are many other things I cannot yet divulge concerning miraculous events which have changed the fates of nations.

People certified dead by responsible physicians have been restored to life after several hours by Baba's touch. Frequently, people have seen him as Shiva, or Rama or Kirshan, but this has always been done for specific spiritual purposes, not for exhibitionism. One dead man was given about a month's 'reprieve' to complete his work of evolution, during which time the poor were given relief and the faith of doubters strengthened. Baba's own father and mother, who died when he was young, were brought in touch with him in their newly born bodies and helped to see their past connections with him in clear visions. They are alive and bear witness to this.

Once, a group of naxalites went to him with the intention of doing him bodily harm—these misguided Bengali youths could not appreciate the role of Baba, the great Bengali saint. They left him after a few days as his staunchy disciples. Many a life has been changed for the better by a mere word or smile smile from him. He exudes Godly confidence and love, none can remain unaffected after coming in contact with him.

I would like to relate some of the experiences I personally have had of the life of Baba Sita Ram Das Onkarnath, each of which left an indelible mark on my mind.

Baba celebrates the four months of Chaturmash from about 15 July to 15 November every year in intense spiritual activity involving a programme of nam sankirtan, recitation from sacred books, such as the Ramayana and the Gita, Sukhmani, Pooja and Arati. Disciples dance in ecstasy around the altar doing hari kirtan, with Baba solemnly leading the party, reminding one of Chaitanya Mahaprabhu. The harmonium, kensis and hridang are all used on this occasion. Phal prasas in the morning and delicious meals at lunch and dinner are served to thousands of people, and sadhus and the poor are properly fed and given a seat of honour. Baba supervises everything, going to each one in turn, and insisting on everyone eating to his heart's content. Lunch finishes about 3 p.m. and after an hour's rest, katha starts. A long but sweet Bengali prayer composed by Baba is repeated three times a day. Nam kirtan and arati follow again, till almost mid-night, when dinner is eaten. Then, while his followers snatch some rest, Baba replies to his heavy mail, mostly by his own hand.

It is a treat to see Baba replying to his mail. Every letter is properly read and all queries answered. Some of the inquiries are spiritual and many are personal, mundane problems. Someone wants Baba to help build a house, find a husband for a daughter, someone a job, or get someone else transferred; others ask his blessings in cases of incurable disease. Some of the letters give great anguish to Baba. He often takes other people's diseases upon himself to relieve the suffering of those without the capacity to bear it themselves. Can there be greater kindness and generosity?

There was a man who brought his only son, who was suffering from double pneumonia, to the feet of Baba and said 'My saviour, I have no one to go to. I am poor. Doctors tell me my son won't live. Please help me.' Baba said, 'Nam karo', meaning Recite God's name, and touched the child, which cured him, but brought the disease upon Baba. The child went home cured by the miracle, but Baba was left lying in bed for two weeks with double pneumonia. In another similar situation, doctors advised Baba to rest, and prescribed drugs. Baba immediately proceeded in a third class compartment to Puri, so that he could visit the Jagannath Temple there and take prasad as his only medicine. Amazingly, he was cured.

Once Baba had synovitis in one knee and was lying in bed in great pain and with a high fever in the house of the late Padma Lochan Mukerjee, a Calcutta industrialist. Mrs Mukerjee, popularly known as 'Lakhima', energetically ensured that no one disturbed Baba in his room. She upbraided the hundreds of men and women gathered outside hoping for darshan and blessings, saying, 'Don't you understand he has a high temperature and is in such severe pain that even to touch his charpoy increases the pain? He won't see anyone. Please go away. Come only when he is better.' Suddenly Baba shouted from his room, 'Don't send them away. Open the doors. Let them come in and meet me.' The doors were thrown open and hundreds poured in, they surrounded Baba on his bed, each one telling his or her own tale of woe. Baba listened intently; blessed each one in turn and said: 'Remember God, all your legitimate desires will be fulfilled.'

I went with my wife to Calcutta at this time to enquire about his health. The doctors had warned me not even to touch his bed since even a slight jerk would increase his pain. On seeing us, Baba smiled his gracious smile and simply said, 'Have you ever heard me singing?' I was taken aback at this strange question and reverently said, I never had the good fortune. Baba immediately began to sing a Bengali song in praise of God. He exuded joy and we were greatly touched by this kindness and amazed at his composure under such circumstances. Childlike, he then said, 'They have recorded a tape of this music. Go upstairs, ask for it and listen to it. You will like it.'

Recently, a panel of eminent Calcutta doctors, who are either his disciples or admirers and who regularly examine him, discovered in an X-ray that Baba had large patches of TB in both lungs. They had examined him two months earlier and found the lungs perfectly clear. They could not understand how this disease could attack Baba so extensively within two months. In their natural anxiety, they advised complete rest and appropriate drugs to which Baba said, 'Can this treatment be delayed one week? During this week, I shall try to clear it myself by meditation. If, in a week's time, you find the disease has not gone, you can start your treatment.' The doctors agreed, but were certain that no amount of meditation could cure TB.

A week later, the X-rays showed both lungs to be clear, to the astonishment of these eminent physicians. All they could then do was to prostrate themselves before him and say 'How can we, with our limited knowledge, understand you, an incarnation? This is your leela, your play.'

A man has told me of the case of his wife. After being chronically ill and bedridden for years, during which time medical treatment had failed to help her, she was on the brink of death when this man, as a last resort, went to the local village temple to pray. On the way, he was thinking of his guru, Baba Onkarnath, perhaps for the first time so intensely, since all his own efforts had failed. On reaching the temple, he found it locked and the priest nowhere to be found. In utter helplessness, therefore, this man lay crying at the temple door in the intense heat of midsummer. Someone touched him, and he opened his eyes to see Baba, standing close by him and asking him to take him to his house in the village. The man touched Baba's feet in gratitude for arriving in the nick of time to save his wife, and led the way back, across the fields, to his village. On the way, there was a big lake, directly in their path. The man walked straight into the water and would have been drowned had he not been saved by some villagers who saw him walk so recklessly into the lake. He talked of Baba whom nobody else had seen. His story of leading Baba to his village through the lake made him seem really mad. Everyone sympathized with him because of his wife's illness and his poverty and, assuming that his distress had caused him to become unbalanced, they took him back to his dying wife in the village.

They were all amazed to find his wife, who had been unable to move from bed, standing outside the house. She was looking for a sadhu who, she said, had come into the house, asking for alms, which she had given, getting up from her bed with great difficulty. Immediately afterwards, the sadhu had disappeared. She had never met Baba, but the sadhu, she described, with long matted hair, a thin bare body and bare feet, was undoubtedly Baba Onkarnath. But where had he gone? Having met both the husband and the wife separately, the proof of his physical presence was unmistakable. As an irrefutable proof, the ailing woman had left her bed and appeared fully recovered. They all stood awe-struck at the powers of this great master, who was, perhaps, a thousand miles away from them by that time.

But something more remarkable happened when my wife

entered a nursing home at Indore for a serious operation. She was naturally very nervous during the evening prior to the operation. I tried to console her, asking her to think of Baba Onkarnath. Nothing appeared to work with her at that time. After promising her that I would be with her before the operation, I went to my bungalow in Mhow Cantonment, but I could not sleep. I kept praying for her. Next morning, when I entered her room in the nursing home, she had been made ready for the operation.

I expected to find her in a state of extreme apprehension. But, to my utter surprise, I found her smiling. She said, 'There's nothing to worry about. Baba was here soon after you left, and assured me all would be well.' I have never known a patient so calm and confident as I saw her prior to her operation. I waited outside the operating theatre, and after the operation the surgeon informed me that, somewhat to his own surprise, the operation had been a great success and that my wife would be able to leave the nursing home after two or three days having previously said it would take seven to ten days. I brought my wife back home in the morning of the fourth day, hale and hearty.

Some years later, she had to undergo a hysterectomy. Baba advised me about certain dates which were suitable for the operation. This time, I was rather nervous. She was very weak already and getting on in age. How would she take such major surgery? However, she was certain, all would be well since Baba knew about it. During the operation, the surgeon found that the appendix also needed immediate removal. In fact, he said that one more day and the appendix would have burst, with serious consequences. However, the operation was a great success, and my wife was home a week later, completely restored. A gynaecological surgeon told me he had never seen anyone make such a quick recovery before.

A retired IG of Police tells everyone how a hernia he had suffered from for seven years disappeared one day when Baba jokingly caught hold of his hand and gave it a sudden jerk.

Perhaps, most amazing is the incident of the illness and 'death' of Padma Lochan Mukerjee in a Medical College Hospital in Calcutta. Mrs Mukerjee had wired to Baba, then at Benares, asking him to go and see her husband in the hospital. Baba then went by air to Calcutta, but on going straighty from the airport to the hospital, he was informed by the matron that Mr Mukerjee had died some time earlier. Baba went to the bed of Padma Lochan Mukerjee and sat silently with his hand on the dead man's chest. After some time, the pulse and the heartbeat returned. Padma Lochan opened his eyes and said, 'Baba, I was being taken away when you arrived and stopped them. I thought it was only a dream. But when I opened my eyes I saw you sitting on my bed. Strange!' All his relatives saw this miracle and the matron tore up the death certificate and said, 'Baba is Christ reborn.' The Principal of the College, along with some professors, became his disciples, and requested Baba to visit all the wards and bless all the patients, which Baba gladly did. This became a daily affair, a round of all the wards and blessings for all. The Calcutta newspapers were agog with this news and recorded all this with lavish praise.

Baba took Padma Lochan Mukerjee home and told him that a short reprieve was granted to him to complete his course of sadhana or spiritual practices so that he could achieve salvation. Baba stayed with him in his house for this period. Nam kirtan went on, twenty-four hours a day. Everything was completed to perfection within a period of about a month, when the noble soul of that great devotee of Baba passed to the higher spheres, as directed by Baba.

I had earlier met Padma Lochan Mukerjee. A rich industrialist blessed with sweet children and a noble wife, Lakhima, he had a large three-stroyed mansion in Ballygunge, Calcutta, every room of which had been converted into a sort of temple with pictures of Baba and deities. He had become a sadhu, entrusting his worldly responsibilities to his brother and sons and went roaming as a common follower of Baba wherever he went. I had spoken to him on the much-discussed subject of his being Baba's father in his previous incarnation about which he had this to say, 'My wife saw herself as being Baba's mother, in a vision she had at the time of initiation at his birthplace. I myself merely felt that the village and the people were familiar, but was not advanced enough to see more.' His wife treated Baba as her own child ever afterwards, often feeding him with her own hands. Baba readily submitted to her affectionate discipline, even though he was then about eighty years old.

II

Baba's bed consists of just one blanket, folded twice, with a pillow made out of a blanket seat, or asan, used at one time by his guru and presented to him as a gift. This bed is invariably laid out in the room or cottage where nam is being chanted all day. Half of the breadth of this already narrow bed is occupied by books, magazines and letters. There is also likely to be an odd cloth bag containing masala which Baba used himself and distributes to everyone after a meal because of its digestive properties. He replies to all Bengali correspondence in his own hand, dictates replies to letters in English or Hindi to an interpreter and has the reply translated back to him to check its accuracy.

When we were preparing Baba's room in the new Rishikesh ashram, we tried to make it as comfortable as our love dictated. Thick, soft carpets covered the floor, the wooden bed had a foam mattress and pillows, and silk sheets. There was a fine mosquito-net, and bedside lights, powered by batteries, were provided in case of an electrical failure. In short, all the comforts that I could think of were provided. Baba was pleased to see the ashram hall, cow-shed with a milk cow, the nam manch, kitchen, the store and everything else. He blessed the ashram and said his prayers sitting on a beautiful carpet within the hall.

After all this, to my great delight, he went to his room and lay down on the bed we had provided for him. However, soon afterwards he got up, saying he could not sleep since the room was too richly furnished. He went straight to his blanket on the floor of the cottage where nam sankirtan was going on and promptly went to sleep. Incidentally, it was raining and the water, leaking through the roof, was close to wetting his blanket, but he was oblivious of this. I was pained to see that he would not use the comforts which with great love, had been provided for his personal use. I left the ashram compound and was pondering this in my tent just outside. Baba sensed all this and sent for me. I rushed up to the nam manch.

He smiled and said, 'I know you won't be able to sleep if I stay here. So, I shall move to my room, provided you can arrange a party to do nam sankirtan in my room also. You know I can't sleep without nam.' I was delighted and soon arranged the kirtan party. This pleasure of mine was short-lived, for hardly had I left Rishikesh for Delhi when he distributed everything to anyone who was in need. On my next visit, I found the room almost bare. Three floor carpets remained, but they were being used by the sadhu disciples, not by Baba.

Some time later, when in Kulu, I saw a beautiful woollen shawl which was light and very warm. I purchased it for Baba and took it to Bethur. Knowing his austere nature, I felt some hesitation in broaching the subject of this present to him, but the cold winds of the severe winter encouraged me to put the shawl round him and I looked at him with the delight of a lover. He graciously accepted it, made much of it by moving round and showing it to all and sundry, saying, 'Look, Sujan has brought this Toosh shawl for me.' Simultaneously, he told a sadhu, 'Let Sujan go, I will give this to you', which he did.

That is Baba. Can you clothe the sun or the moon? No! they shed whatever is not consistent with their nature so that they continue to shine in their pristine glory. Baba is the same; he accepts your adoration and love and passes the gifts on to those in greater need. He is the great giver, one who continues to give without looking at your merit.

A giver goes on giving. Only the recipients get tired of receiving.
*Guru Granth Sahib*

On occasions like his birthday or Pooja celebrations, we have come home laden with gifts and clothes besides spiritual blessings. On one of his birthday celebrations at Mahamillan Math, Calcutta, he decorated me with the biggest triple garland of flowers, from around his neck, and then tied a crown made of golden lace, which some devotee had brought for him, over my turban. He ordered me to stand by his side during those celebrations, the envy of all eyes. I was conscious of my weaknesses, which made this great act of kindness stand out all the more. Who can ever forget such exhilarating love?

All presents brought to him are distributed. All money is spent. There are no bank accounts, the money being spent either on propagation of nam or feeding and looking after the needs of the poor, he would incur debts. You cannot imagine his delight when he is feeding people who look famished and hungry.

At Pushkar, all beggars were given two blankets each by him since they were not satisfied with one. The total ran into hundreds of blankets which cost no small sum. They were also fed sumptuously. The strictest discipline is maintained in his ashrams where no money is ever wasted. Delinquents, drunkards and dacoits, or robbers, are put on the right path and made into decent citizens—drunkards have sworn in his presence never to touch liquor again and have gone back transformed. I have seen a dacoit cutting wood for Baba's kitchen and, although all the sadhus were afraid of him, he himself feared Baba and at no cost was prepared to annoy him.

A senior army officer once went with me to Baba for initiation. However, his wife was not easily convinced of Baba's powers, but subsequently this army officer was despatched on a mission in the mountains, where communication was difficult. For three months, there was no news of him, and since the terrain was full of hazards, his wife was naturally worried.

She went with me to Baba one day to ask him about the safety of her husband, this being the first time she had been keen to test Baba's powers. Chaturmash was being celebrated and Baba met us on the way, going towards Narbada for a bath and to fetch his own share of drinking water from the river.

On seeing her, Baba said, 'Nam karo, all will be well.' I told her that her wish had already been granted by Baba without her explaining the case to him. She said, 'But he has not even heard me and Baba says, "nam karo", to almost everyone. I must meet Baba and explain.' I told Baba all this when he returned from the river and he said, 'I have already met her and told her but she can come to have her say.' She gave the story of her anguish to Baba, who said, 'I have already told you to recite the nam and all will be well.' She was still not satisfied although I assured her on the way home that she need have no more worries. That night she received the first telegram from her husband, saying he was well. Next morning she had nothing but praises for Baba.

Some sceptical people will call the above a coincidence, but I have personally seen so many similar instances that I have no doubt of the unbelievable powers of Baba.

Another incident stands out. My younger son became involved in the indiscipline that shook the administration of his college. A young college boy was run over and killed by a truck which was later burnt by students. The rigid and unsympathetic attitude of the college authorities resulted in a strike and acts of serious recklessness. Then the College Authorities took yet another vicious step and expelled several students from the college, including my son. He was on the verge of completing his education and his expulsion at this stage came as a great shock to my wife and myself. Fortunately, Baba was staying with us at our farm house which we have called 'Onkarnath Dham'. I was hesitant, but my wife almost dragged me to Baba's room and told Baba the whole story. My son had also arrived and was taken along with us to Baba.

Baba abruptly said, 'Who can expel this boy? I sent for him myself since all others in the family have had my darshan and he alone has been deprived of it. He will go back and take his engineering degree.' We felt relieved at once. Next morning, a telegram reached me from the college authorities requesting the boy to be sent back at once to resume his studies. Was this also a coincidence? It is amazing how our minds refuse to be convinced, even after seeing irrefutable proof of these spiritual powers day after day.

I had gone to Benares, to meet Baba after taking a week's leave. Earlier, I had almost gone through hell. Duty had forced me to take severe action against a few corrupt and characterless officers who happened to be quite influential in certain quarters. Severally and jointly they had made life very difficult for me and both myself and my wife passed through an undeserved ordeal, though, possibly, it was a result of our past 'karmas'. Baba had earlier told us that 'God, which is Truth, will protect you', which he did.

Immediately upon my arrival at Baba's ashram in Benares, Baba dispersed all his followers saying, 'I am going into agyatbas, an unknown place, and would not like to be disturbed.' I too felt worried. We had just arrived and if Baba was disappearing into the blue, we should have to return home very disappointed. He sensed this, took me aside and said, 'You will stay with me.' But, I said, 'Baba, I have brought my wife as well.' He said, 'She will also stay with you.' This was most unusual and very heartening, more so, when we learnt that Baba had hired two boats, one for the attendants and the kitchen and the second one for himself where we could also be accommodated. We cruised on the river Ganges at Benares, with Baba as our constant companion, and nam kirtan going on day and night. The food, as usual, was delicious, and the fruit plentiful. Above all, there was heavenly peace, which is natural amidst such a powerful sangam of spiritual forces. We felt rejuvenated. After four days of this exhilerating experience, Baba brought us back to his ashram at Benares and then took me to the Durga Temple.

In the temple, there were just the two of us. I requested Baba to introduce me to Ma Durga. Baba said, 'All right.' 'Ma, this is Sujan. He will be going to war. Protect him and destroy his enemies. Make him a powerful instrument to bring victory to the country.' This was December of 1970. There were no signs of war anywhere, as the trouble in Bangladesh did not start until March 1971. Baba knew what even Sheikh Mujib-ur-Rahman, the great leader of Bangladesh did not know; that there would be a war of liberation in his country. I was to participate in this war, in December 1971 and win one of the highest awards for gallantry, the Param Vishist Sewa Medal, for what Ma Durga did for us on the intercession of Baba. How can this be a coincidence? What actually happened in the war cannot be described here but it proved to me and my command that a force of immeasurable magnitude was working for us, destroying the enemy's will to fight and protecting us like an impenetrable shield.

When the fighting ended, I visited Dacca and was horrified at the anarchical conditions prevailing there. I left for Calcutta and pleaded with Baba that the whole effort of the liberation of Bangladesh would be wasted if the powerful leadership of Bangabandhu was not available to that country. But Sheikh Mujib was languishing in a prison cell from where he could see his own recently dug grave. President Yahya of Pakistan was determined to execute him. In fact, there was no leader of public opinion in Pakistan prepared to spare the life of this remarkable leader, Sheikh Mujib.

Baba accepted my request. He had had an eye operation: therefore his eyes were bandaged and he was lying down in bed. He immediately folded both hands and said 'Mother dear, Mujib is the soul of Bangladesh. How can that country exist without the soul? Release him at once and send him home.' The poetic Bengali couplet he spoke was at once recorded by a follower who gave it to me. I gave it, in turn, to Begum Mujib who was constantly praying to God for his release. She was sceptical but I assured her that her husband would be home soon. On the very day of Baba's prayer, Mr Bhutto, in Karachi, announced his intention of releasing Sheikh Mujib at once. Knowing the personalities then in authority in Pakistan, no one expected any such act of good-will and generosity on their part. Everyone was surprised, therefore, when Mr Bhutto, in a fine act of statesmanship, released the Sheikh and sent him back, via London, to Bangladesh. Was this not a miracle?

There are many more unbelievable incidents of this kind and many more, doubtless, are still in the womb of time. This eighty-four year old Baba is spending all his time in improving the life of nations, not just of one man. He is not a forecaster of events or a teller of fortunes, he is the builder of destiny. Satyuga cannot be far. The architect is already here.

### III

Baba's devotion to his own guru is unparalleled. He served his guru physically throughout the guru's life so faithfully that the whole of his guru's family became very fond of him. But he did more. He was the one who, taking his guru and his guru's wife to his prayer room one day, got them the darshan of God. The guru lay semi-conscious for several days after this and was so awe-struck that he told his wife never in future to offer prasad to this disciple any more, because he was not sure if God himself had not come to them in the shape of this disciple.

Baba carried his guru's wooden sandals on his chest, saying, 'This is my armour'. Baba also takes 'charnamrit', the water poured over the guru's sandals daily, and he shows remarkable respect to all members of guru's family. Incidentally, all ashrams of Baba have been registered in the name of the eldest son of his guruji and there is nothing in his own name or those of his sons'. Guru Mata, his guru's wife, served her husband with great care, and now, very old bears witness, with trembling lips, to that day when Baba showed them the 'darshan of God'. How richly spiritual must this couple have been to have had such a disciple as Baba.

By the age of only twenty-six, Baba had attained the highest spiritual position possible. At Gaya, he met Bhagwan Das, a great sadhuy of the Nanakshahi order, who appears to have influenced him to keep nauna and read the vani of the Sikh gurus, particularly, Sukhmani, Japuji and Rahras, which had been translated into Bengali. Baba read Sukhmani with relish and all his own disciples are enjoined to read this daily. One disciple possesses as a momento, a copy of Sukhmani, every page of which is soaked with Baba's tears.

Some 350 years ago, a great sage of Orissa, named Achytananda prophesied that a great bhakta by the name of Probodhchandra Mukhopadhyaya would be born. Later in his life, he would have one leg damaged. In him the Lord himself would incarnate. He would be the preacher of maha mantra and wear guru's sandals on his chest. The sage went on to say much more about the great spiritual powers of this saint, and how he would protect thousands of his disciples in dangerous times.

Baba is restoring the faith of millions by reviving their old neglected temples and recovering neglected idols and arranging for their daily worship. Baba has even built an ashram at Chitor-mar-parra on the Grand Trunk Road, near

Magra, in Hoogly, a very lonely place, far from any human habitation. Baba said he did this for the deliverance of hundreds of ghosts who pleaded with him. When this ashram was being built, innumerable human skulls were dug out, thus proving conclusively the theme of the ghosts. It was later confirmed that this was a favourite site for highway robbery and murder. He has also built mosques for Moslems who hold him in great esteem, and some forty years ago, he wrote a play with an excellent Moslem theme which was shown to packed Moslem houses by a Moslem dramatic society. Later, it was reprinted and dedicated to Sheikh Mujib.

Baba has been known to have given mantra to animals like cows, and inanimate objects like the paintings of some artists. I have personally known him to ask an eminent disciple to bring the photo of his deceased wife for this purpose. An atheist wanted peace without changing his atheistic conviction, which Baba made possible for him, simultaneously changing his whole outlook. At a railway station, Baba introduced me to a committed communist who had been transformed beyond belief.

Although at the age of twenty-six, Baba was already a Master, he was very sparing in giving initiation. He would lay down difficult conditions necessitating years of practise before accepting a disciple. But on 22 April 1937 while Baba was in Samadhi, Lord Jagannath Deva appeared before him and urged him to give initiation to all men and women who come to him, irrespective of caste and creed. That is how people like myself began availing themselves of the limitless spiritual powers of this great saint.

The diksha or initiation that Baba bestows is called by various names like 'niradhara' or 'jnanvati' or 'vedha diksha'. It is best known as Sidha Yoga, in which the guru infuses his power into the spiritual content of the disciple by touch, look or sound. He charges the mantra with life and it becomes sentient. In the course of time, the dormant kundalini awakens and starts its upward journey without any effort on the part of the disciple, who can enjoy the whole operation as a spectator. No rigorous spiritual exercises and hours of specified postures or control of breath or abstinence are prescribed, only respectful surrender to the guru and the verbal or mental repetition of the mantra at all times or whenever possible.

The Master, while explaining this powerful method of initiation to a disciple, said, 'You are now in a lift. You do not have to worry about the route; nor is any personal effort required, except concentration on the mantra and you will experience jyoti, light, and nad, astral music. Concentrate on nad and the chitta will dissolve, the finite and the infinite will merge'.

There are very few today who can claim to be in a position to give the sidha yoga type of diksha. Privileged are those who can take advantage of Baba while he adorns our world in his physical form.

Although Baba does not prescribe any special discipline, it is amazing how, whatever he has said to you, is recalled several times a day and night, proof that the 'lift' keeps working.

You need not stop your everyday work nor live in a forest. While waiting, or travelling or working one can, without any special effort, repeat the mantra in your mind. It becomes a pleasant habit, dispelling the boredom of tedious work or long journeys. All times of the day and night are good but Baba says twenty-four minutes before and twenty-four minutes after sunrise and at midnight, noon and sunset are the best for concentration since at those times the sushama is working and concentration is easiest.

You need not change your guru, since Baba himself is against it. You can, however, put life into the mantra given by your own guru or your own religion by hearing the same words of the mantra repeated by Baba. This is known as 'mantra chaitanya'.

Many people are spiritually advanced, but very few of them have been nominated by God to act as gurus or buddhas. Gurus have seen God while in their own physical body and are always in touch with Him, and they alone have the power to take others with them to the ultimate reality that is called God.

I and my father are one.
*Jesus Christ*

135

Many Europeans and American men and women come to India hoping to meet accomplished sadhus for their spiritual advancement, but go back disappointed. Many are misled by self-seeking men posing as sadhus and Masters, educated professionals, who, by their mastery of the English language and knowledge of religious literature, can easily sway them. They hardly get an opportunity of meeting the real Masters who mostly have no knowledge of any foreign language, and often lack eloquence, even in Indian language. Spiritualism is a matter of personal experience and coming face-to-face with the truth, a process which needs no logic or philosophy or 'modern education'. Many Europeans who come to Baba will not take prasad or blessed fruit since his disciples distribute this with their bare hands, which they regard as unhygienic.

Some Masters abjure common society, whilst others stay within that society observing all the injunctions of the holy scriptures and setting a perfect personal example. Both types constantly influence society by their powerful spiritual vibrations to change for the better. They may not be difficult to contact but it is extremely hard to identify them as Masters once they are contacted. No wonder, therefore, that westerners hardly ever get a chance of coming near them. I remember many westerners who used to visit Baba at his Rishikesh ashram. One old French lady would be permeated with joy on meeting Baba, who said she was filled with God, hence the joy she exuded. There was a young English boy named David Brian Farley, who was hardly sixteen, shy and reserved but very sincere and had met several sadhus. Baba somehow attracted him and he came to stay at Baba's ashram where Baba initiated him, and he became a true vegetarian. He would join the sankirtan party with a pair of nensis given to him by Baba and sing and dance in real devotion. He left for London via Kabul, and wrote to Baba of the miraculous escapes he had had on this hazardous journey. He continues to write to 'Mother' and adores Baba.

There was an American lady, rather plump and always wore ochre robes, who was disgusted with some of the gurus she had met. She asked me to ask Baba if there was no one in India who could give her the spiritual satisfaction she had come to India to find . . . She said it was no use taking initiation since it was all a hoax. She was really blunt, for which I do not blame her after the experiences she had had with some of our educated frauds.

Baba listened to all this attentively and asked me to tell her to come the next day at dawn, if she wanted to have the experience, to which she gladly agreed. Next morning, Baba asked me to take her to the cowshed, make her sit on a woollen blanket provided by the ashram and do japa or repetition of guru nam. This I did and a few minutes later, Baba went with me into the cowshed, stood behind her and, giving a mantra asked her to repeat it within his hearing so that there was no mistake in pronunciations. She said the mantra given by Baba could not be a proper one, since she had been told by some Masters that every mantra must have the word 'aum' as a constituent part of it. Baba laughed and said whoever told her this did not know even the alphabet of spiritualism. Baba said very few people are entitled to have aum in their mantras. Those who are not so entitled, or anadhikari, would go mad if they repeated such a mantra. I explained all this to her and at the same time told her that however brilliant the patient, he is always well advised to leave the prescription to the physician. She agreed and then sat with eyes closed. Baba now pressed his thumb onto the middle of her forehead and asked her to repeat the mantra after him, which she did. Baba instructed her to keep sitting and concentrate on the sound of the mantra as repeated by herself, until he came back. Then he and I left her for a few minutes. When we went inside again, Baba asked her through me if she had experienced anything. She said, 'Yes, I have got what I was after. Firstly, there was some force welling up within my body which was so overwhelmingly powerful that I thought I could not bear it and I would burst. But ,then through Baba's kindness it settled down into a deep and inexpressible peace and joy.' She asked me to ask Baba if he could also reduce her weight as she was very conscious of her figure. I told Baba this and all of us laughed heartily.

One American Jew was initiated by Baba and he stayed for a long time in the ashram sincerely following all he could understand. He had left the ashram of Maharishi Mahesh

Yogi, owing to some differences.

The military camps located adjacent to Baba's ashram were so influenced by Baba, who would lovingly invite and feed hundreds of soldiers on festive occasions such as Durga that they gave up drinking and started nam sankirtan in their off-duty hours. Their officers noticed that the discipline and sense of duty of these soldiers improved remarkably.

Police Officers of the highest rank have become Baba's disciples and, through their influence, many policemen have started taking interest in singing God's name in their units, and leading the clean lives of religious people. This is no small miracle. How I wish the Indian Government would utilize the immense powers of this saint by inviting hi mto address all Government establishments and transforming their very nature.

## 22

# *The Philosophy and the Methods*

# *of Spiritual Evolution*

It may sound strange, but a person only uses about a millionth part of his mental powers during his lifetime. Only the lower centres are activated, since they are concerned with the individual's daily needs, and are fed by external stimuli; to which the senses of sight, smell, taste, touch and hearing, have to respond. The ego is the commander of these senses and also the recipient of the fruits, good or bad, since people judge everything by their own experience and take action in accordance with their preconceived ideas. Some of the latter are legacies of past births or sanchit karmas. By daily exercise, these sense instruments get so powerful, that they dominate the whole thinking process of an ordinary individual, starting the chain of cause and effect and the perpetual cycle of births and deaths.

God has endowed man with such tremendous potential that, when aroused, nothing is beyond man's capabilities. But millions have never heard of these powers which are known only to a limited number of the initiates of spiritually evolved saints and yogis. A common man often finishes his earthly sojourn in utter misery, unaware of his rich inheritance:

> Our condition may be likened to a prince who, while sleeping on his throne, dreams himself to be a beggar.
>
> *Guru Granth Sahib*

> How little do we know that which we are;
> Still less that what we may be!
> *Byron*

God has so constituted man that he is a microcosm, and our scientific knowledge of the human body is limited to what we can physically perceive. The spiritual scientist, however, knows of the existence of physical, astral and causal bodies in each individual, as well as the presence of twenty-two psychic centres, which put man in touch with various astral worlds, about which common people know little. No wonder, therefore, that even those noble souls who are dedicated to God or awareness of the Inner Being, fall prey to the superficialities of their father's religion and, at best, merely lead exemplary lives of selflessness and service to humanity, though this binds them further to the cycle of the karma, denying them the liberation which is their birthright.

It may be fruitful at this stage to give a description of the various psychic centres as an introduction to this fascinating subject. It should be stressed, however, that the activation of these centres, whether by patanjilli or yoga methods or by any other method is a matter of personal aptitude and choice and has to be done under the loving supervision of an accomplished guru, without whom training is dangerous and should be avoided.

## KUNDALINI SHAKTI

Kundalini shakti, the residual power, lies curled up like an inverted snake at the indri chakra near the sacral plexus, and when activated, shoots up through the central canal of the spinal cord to the brain. If the body is not prepared for such 'high voltage', a man can go insane or even die. Hatha Yoga systems have a tendency to force the process, even when the body is not ready, resulting in disastrous consequences to the disciple.

## LOWER PSYCHIC CENTRES

Yogis normally commence their concentration on the lowest of the psychic centres, the muladhara or guda chakra, which is shaped like a lotus flower with four petals.

The second chakra in ascending order is indri chakra, situated near the sacral plexus, where kundalini shakti lies coiled up, and is shaped like a lotus with six petals.

The third is nabhi chakra, situated near the solar plexus, the umbilicus, and is a lotus with eight petals.

Fourth is hridaya chakra near the cardiac plexus, the heart, and is a lotus with twelve petals.

Fifty is kanth chakra near the cervical plexus, the throat, and is a lotus with sixteen petals.

Sixth is the two-petalled lotus situated at the back of the eyes and on a level with the lower part of the eyeballs. This is said to be the seat of the mind and the soul.

Seventh is a four-petalled lotus just above the sixth one which provides the four mental faculties of mana, buddhi, chitt and ahankar.

The number of petals up to the seventh chakra, add up to fifty-two. Each petal is said to have a peculiar musical note which can be heard by a yogi whose inner hearing has been activated. This is also the maximum that the human vocal chords can reproduce. Rishis constituted the fifty-two letters of Sanskrit alphabet based on these notes which they could hear and decipher easily. Thus, even language became a vehicle for spiritual advancement.

Human consciousness generally remains confined within the bounds of the above psychic centres, or chakras, and the nerve centres connected with the corresponding parts of the brain. Unless a determined effort is made to raise consciousness progressively to the remaining fifteen psychic centres, it cannot enter the astral worlds. This is the dividing line and the 'tenth gate' between the physical and astral, which cannot be crossed easily, but once it is penetrated, there is no limit to a man's power; he fathoms all secrets and finds everything at his command.

## THE TENTH GATE

The human body has nine gates which open outwards and only one that opens inwards and it is this tenth and the most important one which, not unnaturally, has been kept secret:

Nine doors He made explicit,
the tenth one He kept Secret.
*Guru Granth Sahib*

The nine doors are:
Two eyes

141

Two ears
Two nostrils
The mouth
The sex organ
The rectum

If consciousness continues to flow out of these doors, there is never enough strength to penetrate the tenth door which needs the concentrated effort of complete consciousness before it can be opened. The whole effort, therefore, of all yoga systems is to close the outer gates and to open the inner one. Mostly, the breath or prana is utilized for this purpose by the hatha yogis. It is obvious that any error in the use of this tremendous energy can wreck the physical body. The awakening of the kundalini by this process can set a person on fire, so that even complete burial in snow does not extinguish the inner heat. All astral and spiritual worlds lie beyond these psychic centres and the tenth gate.

## THE PHYSICAL ASTRAL AND SPIRITUAL UNIVERSE

Beyond the physical worlds which consist predominantly of matter energized by spirit, there are the astral worlds composed of highly refined matter with a great proportion of spirit. The universal mind is located there. Beyond these are the worlds of pure spirit, whilst in between, there are mixtures of various kinds and categories. It is clear that the soul in its upward journey, has to be as refined as the constituents of the worlds it has to visit, otherwise it has no chance of getting there. At every stage, there is a kind of a sieve whose holes become progressively finer. All dross has to be left behind.

The attachment to men and material is a load which cannot pass through the 'sieve'.

Blessed are the poor in spirit; for theirs
is the kingdom of heaven.

*Lord Jesus*

Similarly, ungratified desires act as a downward pull. Unless the desire to go up is much stronger than the opposite attraction, no progress can be made. Love is the most powerful and positive force for spiritual progress, in particular Love of God. But love cannot be artificially generated, particularly when the object to be loved is not within easy reach of the physical senses and has never been seen or heard by the individual concerned. One takes the bounties of God for granted; air and water; the sun, the moon and the stars; cereals, vegetables and fruits, are all life-sustaining and delightful but who thinks of thanking the invisible Creator? The children whose rich parents have had them brought up by paid nurses and servants hardly show their parents any affection, even though they owe every comfort of their lives to them. For the generation of love, contact with the object of that love is a vital necessity. Since God is pure, unalloyed spirit, only a spirit has a chance of direct contact with God. It is the intense love for God alone which induces an ordinary mortal to undertake the back-breaking task of converting himself into a spirit, a commitment that may take a whole lifetime, even several lifetimes. Very few, therefore, undertake this task. Those few are pre-destined, and in their case, several births have taught them the transistory nature of worldly pleasures and only then do they start looking for the real source of perpetual joy.

When the chela is ready, the guru appears.
*Indian saying*

The mere fact that one in several thousands answers the call shows clearly that he has been called because he is ready. He appears to have inherited Love of God. This feeling of love is further heightened to the exclusion of all else, by his contact with the most devout and committed saints who appear from nowhere and attract him. These saints act as an inspiration as well as a guide.

The perfect Master meets him and takes him to God.
*Guru Granth Sahib*


## ASTRAL PSYCHIC CENTRES

Let us now discuss the fifteen psychic centres which deal with the astro-spiritual world, of which the first in the line is called shiva-netra or trikuti and is located at a point midway between the two eyebrows.

The next one, a little above the first, is the eight-petalled lotus and next higher one is the sahasra-dal kanwal, which is considered the real centre of the astral world. The next ones continue progressively higher until they reach the top part of the cranium.

Some systems advocate concentration on one centre at a time till it is seen with closed eyes and its musical notes are properly heard. Progress is slow and, perhaps, the short span of human life is not adequate to complete the process. Others suggest daily concentration on each and every centre so that the whole system is activated simultaneously. Mostly, however, only three centres, Nabhi chakra, hridaya chakra and shivanetra chakra are chosen for practising concentration, some systems favouring one and some another. Radhaswamis advocate concentration on shivanetra or trikuti at the very commencement and consider this a shortcut in the yoga process. There is much to be said for this theory.

## THE PIERCING OF THE SHEATHS

Baba Onkarnath, in his book *Birahnir Abhisar*, or Sidha Yoga, mentions that when a guru, in his mercy, grants sidha yoga to his disciple, the kundalini shakti is activated. It then sets about breaking the coverings of the sthula or physical, sukshma or astral, and karna or spiritual bodies so that the soul can be freed to merge with God. The sthul body has its centre at Brahm Granthi, the 'Root of the Supreme' in the navel. Piercing this body is accompanied by the shaking of the body, palpitations, creeping sensations near the spine, head nodding and the twitching of the body as if it was being pricked by needles. Something snaps within the ear, one dances and roars. All this is outside the control of the individual. The physical body is being automatically purged and purified. Doctors, unable to comprehend this process, may treat it as paralysis agitans.

From this position the kundalini moves to the great void or sunyakasa, which is the heart. The anhad nad, the unstruck

144

sound is heard by the individual at this stage.

The next knot which is the centre of sukshma deha is called Vishnu granthi and lies in the throat. This is also called atisunya. At this stage, bheri nad, a musical instrument, is heard by the yogi, all of which physicians may understand as hallucination.

Finally, the jundalini pierces the rudra granthi, the knot of rudra which is akasa, at the centre of the eyebrows and then the soul is merged with its Lord.

First, each element of the physical body is cleansed of its dross by the kundalini which resides in that element till the process is completed. Only then will it move to the next element. When it takes to earth, the body becomes very stiff; when it takes to water, tears flow automatically; when it takes to fire, there is sweat; when it takes to air, one shivers and the hair stands on end. When it stays in ether, the result is dissolution. Doctors can never understand this condition and will treat it as a disease.

When the kundalini moves to vishnu granthi and starts purging the sukshma deha, transcendental forms of sound, touch, smell and taste are experienced, and visions of lights and deities are seen. Nada of various kinds is also heard, nada which is the supreme being and gives an ineffable ecstasy of joy. Purification of sukshma deha is achieved by nada and jyoti, the combination of sound and light. Ultimately, when the soul merges with its Lord, samadhi, complete absorption, ensues. This is perfection. This is liberation while still in the physical body. The proof is so overwhelming and universal that it leaves no room for doubt. The mere 'feeling good' of an orthodox religious man is no comparison with such a concrete evidence of God. The presence of a living but accomplished guide, whether called satguru, saint, sadhu or Master, is vital at every stage of spiritual development. Only they who have experienced them, can interpret these sights and sounds:

> If a hundred moons went up
> And a thousand Suns rose,
> Even in such enormous light,
> Intense darkness would prevail without a Guru.
> *Guru Nanak*

Bhakti Yoga is considered the safest, though, perhaps, the longest way home. The stress is on love of God. If you love anyone you think of that person constantly, even if you are involved in other activities. Repetition of his Name, any name that appeals to your mind and is in harmony with it, will keep your thoughts constantly centred on God. The very sound of that name has to be in harmony with your nature and your ideal, and it is for this reason that the Masters are in the best position to suggest the Name you should remember God by, which will be different in different cases and in accordance with the predominant tatwas or constituents in a man's nature.

In some people, water predominates, in others earth, in still others, fire; in some ether, in some air. Different deities personify these tatwas and their mantras are brought into play. The whole purpose behind this process of selecting a suitable name and characteristic is to put you in harmony with your ideal, so that you can achieve 'one pointedness', or yak sui, of the mind, which promotes greater powers of concentration. Some people find the abstract names, which do not specify any particular characteristic or guna of God, more in harmony. Aum is one such word, Allah and God are equivalent versions. An ordinary man would find concentration on such abstract Names extremely difficult, if not impossible, but there are some people who believe in a nirgun or one without attributes, God, and are able to concentrate on abstract names. A rosary may be of use in the initial stages, since it helps one carry out a planned programme of japa, the repetition of the name and it reminds one constantly of God and helps in forming a habit of japa. The better method is to form a habit of saying the name with each inhaling and exhaling of breath. This makes one independent of the rosary and one can do more japa.

The constant repetition of the Lord's Name repels all other thoughts which are responsible for creating a wall between God and the Self, a wall of ego which grows thicker and thicker with time, ultimately burying the soul completely under its dead weight.

How does the repetition of the Lord's Name help?

(a) Firstly, it keeps the mind busy and on the right track; it repels undesirable thoughts.

(b) The sound intonation of the selected names stirs up the vibrations of which the body is composed and makes it audible to the inner hearing apparatus, so constituting nad.

(c) It is excellent practice for concentration.

(d) It slowly but surely destroys the ego.

(e) It cleanses the body for the arrival and establishment of nam.

> The ego is opposed to nam
> Both cannot stay together in one place.
> *Guru Granth Sahib*

Therefore, if we wish to have nam residing in our body, the ego will have to vacate the site. The name must be something concrete and tangible for which we have to eject the ego, if we are to make room for it. It cannot be the name or mantra one repeats in japa:

> The whole universe came into existence through nam;
> Without a true guru nam cannot be contacted.
> *Guru Granth Sahib*

The repetition of the Name given by the Guru at the time of initiation, is akin to a flute-like instrument, the been, whose musical notes attract the snake or the nam, and make him dance to the tune. The repetition of Nam causes 'obsession' of the mind and a constant concentration which sharpens the astral instruments of the senses. These instruments in turn, put one in touch with all the phenomena of the astral worlds. Incomparable sights are seen, indescribable music is heard, an exquisite fragrance comes from nowhere and sometimes is even smelt by companions who are not engaged in the effort. One tastes amrit, nectar, whose unique flavour cannot be described. A sensation of joy permeates all the cells of the body, making one's hair stand on end.

When the whole body has been cleansed of all undesirable tendencies and is ready to receive the Lord, then He comes as the 'Holy Ghost' the nam. This is a musical note or a definite Word clearly pronounced at regular intervals. It is distinct, and phrases like guru, guru; waheguru, waheguru; ram, ram; aum, aum; sohand, sohang, are clearly heard inside. This 'Word' is the real nam. One's ears play no part in hearing this sound which appears to be coming over from the right side of the brain and vibrates through the whole bodt. There is no further need for the yogi to repeat the Lord's name as given by the guru. God himself has responded in his kindness and grace and has set everything in motion; the name that now resounds is in complete harmony with the bodily vibrations and continues to hold the attention of the yogi twenty-four hours a day. The music of these notes, whether instrumental or vocal, is so attractive that the mind constantly loves to dwell on it. All doubts are now removed and the astral body is in touch with its astral centre and there is peace and joy. In course of time the 'karna sharir', the very soul, will merge with God and that will be the end of the journey.

Once a loving physical contact has been established with a living saint or guru, and the guru has accepted the responsibility for the chela through initiation, a satguru has the power to guide the chela from within. The guru and the disciple establish complete harmony and get psychologically in touch with each other. At this second stage, the physical presence of the guru is no longer necessary, as the guru's word, the beej mantra given at initiation, has taken root inside the body of the disciple and acts as a constant guide.

Those who are so blessed by the guru, get direct commands, or hukum, which they can clearly hear and understand. Written commands are shown to them in a vision in the language they understant, and if they obey these commands implicitly, they never come to grief. The all-wise spirit, the spirit of guidance, is now guiding every activity of the chela, fulfilling all legitimate desires:

> Obey the command so that you are accepted.
> Then alone you will enter the palace of thy Lord.
> *Guru Granth Sahib*

These are the milestones along the path of spiritual progress which clearly indicate to the disciple that he is on the right track. If you get this guidance daily, if the nam is resounding in your body, if you experience the vision of the spiritual worlds and are intoxicated with it as if you were drunk, then you are thrice blessed and are on the right path. Mere good feeling after recitation of sacred hymns or the performance of noble deeds may not mean much; you may be miles away from the real thing.

> The intoxication of Nam,
> Stays with me day and night.
> *Guru Granth Sahib*

The attractions of the inner life are very powerful and they automatically break the bonds of attachment to worldly things. You find your eternal companion and never wish to leave His company. At this stage, every thing mundane assumes its correct value, since you have had all these illusions removed. You know now your true relationship with near and dear ones as well as opponents and enemies and you fully realize your duties to man and God. Excesses and over-indulgence are painful, and are therefore avoided. Humility takes the place of the ego since you take on a passive role in which you are purely an instrument thus making you humble and ever-dependent on the grace of God. You become fearless, having no anxieties of any kind. If the power rests in the hands of your father who loves you, why should there be any worry? You find you love meditation, and enjoy this more than anything else on earth. Death holds no fear for you, since you leave your physical body daily and return to it at will. This is jeeven mukti, the liberation whilst still in the physical body.

Bhakti or Nam simran under the guidance of an accomplished saint is the safest of all spiritual paths and has been termed 'the Royal Road to God'. Through this process, powers are transferred to the yogi in well-regulated stages so that he is abler to carry them with ease, causing him to become so contented and peaceful even in the early stages, that he is never in a hurry. The intensity of his desire to see God and unite with him increases by his daily practice but he is convinced that His grace will descend, the moment he is ready for it, which is judged by God himself. All doubts cease, success is certain and time is of no consequence. This path is also called Sahaj Yoga, Sahaj being translated as 'slow and spontaneous' or in 'God's own time'.

The initial stage of nam simran, the repetition of name, is naturally dry but the interest in it increases with time and after experiencing the signs which are like milestones on a long journey, It is like sinking a well; initially digging is just drudgery. But one has to perservere, and in due course, the dampness of the soil shows water is close at hand. Then you get mud, and finally pure, life-giving water. Many are disappointed because they do not strike water at the depth at which it was predicted. Instead, they hit rock, which needs determination and effort to break, an effort which has to be greatly increased. But if the soil contains water, the ultimate success is not in doubt. If through sheer lack of determination or lack of faith, a seeker stops the effort, he naturally does not deserve God's grace in the form of water.

Hundreds, even thousands of saints have certified from their own experience that God exists and can be found by their prescribed methods. The need, therefore, is to believe in a spiritual scientist or a saint, who generates maximum faith in you, and then start digging according to his advice. If your love is genuine and not transistory, the result is a foregone conclusion.


## THE CHOICE OF THE GUIDE

A warning note ought to be sounded here in the matter of choosing a guide. Too many people are on the market as gurus. Their number has increased enormously as it is a well paid profession today. A little knowledge of spiritualism, some knowledge of English, a respectable or a weird countenance and the man is off to America or Europe as the top-most yogi guru. Amongst knowledgeable people, a man's avarice, his habits, his girth from over-eating, will give him away. Many can talk well and leave you spell-bound, many have acquired powers after limited tapasya to perform some supernatural acts. This brand has the greatest following today in India as well as elsewhere, but you will get nowhere with this type of guru.

Try to find someone who is sparsely clothed, barefooted, who neither eats nor sleeps too much; who gives away more than he gets daily and is known always to do so, who talks little but who remains constantly immersed in God and is love, personified. He will speak the truth, no matter how much it hurts some egos. His very presence will be elevating and soul-satisfying, and in his presence you will forget all your worries. He will be the support of the poor, whom he will love more than those who are better placed in life. There will never be a word of censure on his lips against any faith or any individual. You will develop respect and love for him, a love that will be so intense that you will be driven to distraction if you cannot meet him as often as you like. If you ever find one like him, never leave him; he is the guru who is a personification of God. If, through some misfortune, you cannot contact such a one, it is better to do without a guru, since a false one is worse than none at all.

My belief is that the true followers, those who imbibe the teachings of the Guru Granth Sahib will be greatly helped by placing themselves at the feet of saints who have been well defined in that sacred book. They will discover the spiritual greatness of the Guru Granth Sahib only after they begin to get exquisite practical experiences, while inebriated with guru bani. The truth that the Guru Granth Sahib is the embodied guru in the Kaliyuga will become crystal clear to them.

The question arises, how to select the true guide. many lay claims to this knowledge. How can we assess their authenticity when we ourselves are so ignorant about this subject? A wrong choice may ruin our whole life.

One neither finds God nor the company of the beloved
And misses the fruits of this world and the next.
*Guru Granth SAhib*

In my view, the Divine Plan is foolproof and depends upon the 'law of attraction and repulsion'. You will be attracted only to these attributes which you yourself desire and, there-fore, value, and will be repelled by those who are repugnant to your taste. Only a square peg will go into a square hole. There can be a misguided effort, but it will soon become clear that the two just will not fit.

God has placed many 'supermen' of all kinds in our midst, thousands of Buddhas, each with his own doctrine. There are yogis who merely concentrate on acquiring supernatural powers; there are saints who shun these powers deliberately and attempt to merge with the very source of all powers. They do not attempt to gather some of the spectacular powers of a yogi, as their goal is to inherit the Divine kingdom, in which some have been known to succeed.

> I and my father are one
> *Lord Jesus Christ*

The story is told of two brothers, one of whom spent all his life with a yogi in the jungle, who taught him the technique of walking on water. This exhibition by the yogi guru was so exciting that this poor man spent all his life, like his guru, in mastering this supernatural feat. The other brother spent his time in business and made himself prosperous and respected. The yogi brother came home after many years and boasted to his brother of the supernatural powers he had acquired. To demonstrate, he took his brother, and other friends and relatives, to a river where, with great ease, he walked straight across to the other bank and back again, to the astonishment and awe of all present. At this stage, his worldly brother said he had acquired powers which were far greater than those of his yogi-brother, all the while enjoying the comforts of a family life. Everyone thought he was joking, but he was serious. He ordered a boatman close by to ferry all those present across the river, at the nominal fare of one paisa each. The boat was soon loaded, and everyone, including the yogi, crossed to the other side and back. All this cost the worldly brother less than half a rupee. Turning to his yogi brother, he said, 'I cannot understand why you spent all your life learning something which can be so easily purchased by any common man?' The yogi brother felt greatly embarrassed. It was evident that through giving in to his own ego, he had contacted the type of guru who could best satisfy that urge.

An urge based upon human desires will make one look for

someone who can fulfil those desires, which betray the character of the man. A child will pursue toys; maturity brings desires consistent with mental development. The final stage is:

I do not desire either kingdom or salvation
I desire your personal Love.
I ask for Thee — all else is full of misery.
Bestow thy contentment giving Nam to satisfy my hunger.
*Guru Granth Sahib*

O Kabir! Your mind is purified like the water of the Ganges.
Now God himself is after you, calling you by your very name.
*Kabir*

A stage of selflessness can have no other goal than achieving the pure spirit of God himself. A beginner can only start with the kindergarten and progress upwards from there, stage by stage, class by class.

Do not laugh at idol worshippers. All of us are so made that we have to have an image even of abstract things before we can understand them properly. The ego, formed by the circumstances of our birth, forces many people to adopt an abstract philosophy they can never understand. They prefer to die in that delusion rather than set out in search of truth. God has so arranged matters that a man can do without Him for a considerable length of time.

We look at each other in our different stages of development and laugh at each other, basing our judgement of the other person only on the one visible image in a long chain of evolution. The Divine design is deliberately slow but foolproof. We have seen how the urge of the disciple based on his past and present desires takes him to an appropriate guru. Each will, therefore, look for special characteristics in his guide, depending on his aim. Here, only those spiritual qualities in a guru which the author of this book considers essential from his own point of view, have been described and, inevitably, they may differ from what some of the readers may find important.

# THE GURU

The word guru means 'the enlightener', the one who dispels the darkness of human ignorance. The greatest ignorance of the human being in its involvement with matter is to feel that it is separate from the ultimate reality. In other words, in the illusions of the world or maya, the individual forgets his identity as a 'royal prince' and goes about begging from door to door in his own kingdom. In this world of illusion, almost everyone is in the same position except those who are holding on to the apron strings of God and whilst enjoying all the sights and scenes of the world, remain in constant touch with the ultimate reality. Only those who are immersed in Truth can guide us to it, not those who, however noble and wise, have no contact with it.

Yogis who had held long discourses with Guru Nanak wanted to exhibit the superiority of the supernatural powers they possessed as an argument in favour of their Hatha Yoga methods. They invited Guru Nanak to accompany them to Hardwar for the Kumbh Mela festival, but they lamented that since Guru Nanak was unable to fly and as they would be flying to Hardwar by means of their Yoga techniques, they could not accompany each other. They tauntingly added that walking to Hardwar would take him months while they would be there in hours, to which Guru Nanak made no response. During their flight, however, the yogis noticed that a pair of wooden sandals was accompanying them. On reaching Hardwar, they found Guru Nanak already seated on the banks of the Ganges. Astonished, they asked him how he had managed to arrive earlier than they did. He replied, 'I live with God who is everywhere. I, therefore, have only to think of the place and I am there in the twinkling of an eye. No effort is needed.' He added that he had sent his wooden sandals to accompany them. It is said that he deflated the ego of many yogis present and some of them became his followers.

## CONSTANT CONTACT WITH GOD

The first requirement in a guru is whether he is in constant contact with God. It is said that Guru Nanak spent all his time singing Gods' praises, meditating on His name and guiding other people along the same path. He said:

> I live only by remembering you
> The moment I forget you I die.
> *Guru Granth Sahib*

If you come across a saint who lives in this manner, run to him, for men of his calibre are rarely born.


## LOVE

A transparent quality in the Guru is 'Love', Love for all beings and things, irrespective of caste, creed or station in Life, Love for animals and men, for trees and stones. God is Love, and this quality has to be paramount in the guru.


## THE SUPERMAN

Fearlessness, self-assurance, equanimity and vairag, or non-attachment, are also essential in a Guru. Wisdom, perfection, love of truth and honesty are other qualities which such a superman will show.


## IMPACT

If you stand on a snow-covered mountain you will be aware of the cold. Similarly, when you meet a saint, you will at once feel peaceful; the vibrations are too powerful not to have an immediate impact. If, however, you go to him in a 'drunken' state, drunk with liquor, or money or pride in worldly achievements, then your contact has to be longer before the appropriate effect is felt. The wall of the ego has first to be broken, for which the true guru has the requisite technique. He may shock you and this may even be unpleasant, but if you want to be cured of this worst of all disease, you will be well-advised to take his medicine, no matter how unpleasant. Sometimes, false pride and an inflated ego will keep a man from the only 'oasis' in the desert and thus a whole lifespan of spiritual progress may be wasted.

The spiritual aspirtant has to have a living guide whom he can consult regularly, since problems occur all too frequently along this path, and even the best of men have to consult somebody.

Ramakrishna Paramhansa once felt an intense burning sensation all over his body. He immersed himself for hours in the cold water of the Ganges, but to no effect. Doctors could not cure him. But Bhairvi, that remarkable lady, who was staying with Paramhansa at the time, told him that Radha and Chaitanya had suffered the same ailment during their austerities, and that the holy scriptures prescribed sufferers to put on a fragrant garland of flowers and apply sandalwood paste to the whole body. Ramakrishna followed this prescription and was cured in three days.

# 23

## The Disciple

Do you imagine that we have created you without purpose and that you would not be brought back to us? Exalted is Allah, the true king. There is no God but He, the lord of the Glorious Throne.

*The Holy Koran.* 23:115, 116.

There are certain prerequisites for the pursuit of any objective. Naturally, the more precious the object of desire, the higher the price it commands. The objective of self-fulfilment is the highest goal anyone can set for himself and, therefore, one should be prepared to pay the highest price for this laudable aim.

> To him that overcometh will I grant to sit with me in my throne, even as I also overcame and am set down with my father in his throne.
>
> *Lord Jesus*

> But a man of disciplined mind, who serves among the objects of the senses, with the senses under control and free from attachment and aversion, he attains purity of spirit.
>
> *Bhagavad Gita*

It is through a perfect guide or guru that we hope to attain self-fulfilment. But, only a deserving chela or disciple is entitled to, and has reasonable chances of contacting a perfect guru. We must clearly understand that a man has to rise above his intellect in order to experience the higher, or shall we say, the finer phenomenon. The physical body has also to be conditioned so that it assists the ascent of the soul into the astral and then the spiritual worlds. All obstacles have to be removed by the disciple to clear the passage for this upward journey, which obstacles are physical, environmentak, psychological and basic.

## PHYSICAL OBSTACLES

The body is to be treated as a temple and kept clean and healthy in preparation for that great day when God, in His mercy, shall descend into it and fulfil all our desires. The body, though built like a fort, is constantly under attack by five powerful enemies.

### 1 SEX (KAM)

Sexual indulgence can not only weaken the physique when done to excess, but can also effect one's capabilities of perseverence, selflessness and determination, weakening the powers of concentration. It can give rise to many problems which will take a whole lifetime to solve. Designed for procreation, sex has become a pastime and a craze which ruins those who indulge in it with lust. Its proper use is nowhere prohibited, and in fact, grihasth ashram, the householder's life, is supposed to be best whilst progressing along the spiritual path. Even in married life, sexual restraint is recommended not only for physical health but because a small family has fewer problems.

The man has first to get rid of the beast in himself, and sex is the worst of the beasts in man. Man's imagination constantly feeds this desire, which then observes no seasons as followed by even the beasts. Some weak-minded but well-intentioned sadhus have gone to the extent of cutting off their sexual organs, with a view to eliminating sexual desire, but extreme violence of this kind generally has quite the reverse effect.

Today's so-called modern civilization is already paying the price of sexual over-indulgence which, like every other weakness, is spreadinl rapidly throughout the world. Even in a religious country like India, sex films and pornographic literature are destroying the very foundations of Indian culture, by encouraging debates and freedom of sex amongst all who can afford it.

The spiritual apprentice, therefore, will be better off if he is a family man but in full control over his desires. Bachelors are not debarred, though their task, in some ways, becomes more difficult.

## 2 ANGER (KRODH)

From anger arises bewilderment, from bewilderment, loss of memory and from loss of memory, the destruction of intelligence and from destruction of intelligence, he perishes.

*Ghagavad Gita*

Anger accompanies hatred, and has no place near love. In anger, a man loses his balance and his judgement is impaired and as it is impossible for him to concentrate on anything, he behaves in a most abnormal manner. I have known a poor man tear off his own shirt daily in anger, without it having any perceptible effect on his opponents. The consequence of anger can only be disastrous for the person who indulges in it.

Sex and anger dissolve the body,
Just as fire melts gold.

Sex and anger are the two most disastrous enemies of mankind and have to be sublimated, not by violence but by positive stress on their opposite virtues.

Higher and selfless love is the answer to both these problems; due and holy respect for mothers, sisters and daughters makes one see other women in their true image and, at once, sublime thoughts take the place of unhealthy ones.

Satwik or pure vegetarian food, avoidance of undesirable company, films and literature, also help a great deal in eradicating these two vices.

## 3 AVARICE (LOBH)

Over-accumulation of wealth, over-eating and similar tendencies add to the worries of man. They do not give any pleasure after the initial act. Because of the effort made to collect, grab or store, attachment to these useless articles grows, making life more miserable. It acts as a downward pull and does not allow the soul to soar higher.

## 4 OVER-ATTACHMENT (MOH)

Over-attachment to one's wife, children, friends, wealth or other possessions, even to one's own body, is unhealthy and is a cause of sorrow and despair. There is a certain amount of natural attachment without which the world would cease functioning but this is not the meaning of 'moh'. It is over-attachment which is bad, and is to be avoided.

## 5 EGO (AHANKAR)

The ego is the root cause of all actions in this world and canot be avoided. But when the ego gets too inflated, overbearing and proud, it becomes dangerous for oneself as well as society. Humility has to be developed by the disciple, a virtue to which Guru Nanak gave great importance. Succeeding gurus followed suit, with humility becoming the hallmark of the Sikh gurus. Selfless public service was enjoined upon rich and poor alike to develop humility. Even now you will find some of the richest sikhs dusting the shoes of all and sundry in the temples, rich sikh ladies, who never do any work at home, washing and cleaning utensils used by the poorest of the poor, at the temple's free kitchen. The ego has been considered by the saints as the greatest barrier in the spiritual path; it is the ego which functions through the confused mind of an individual, adding to his own problems in the belief that it is resolving them. If the ego could only act as the instrument of the supermind, which it actually is, it would get the necessary guidance from the supermind and assist the soul in its upward journey, besides allowing a man to carry out his duties in life more efficiently. But under the belief that it is the originator of a person's every action, the ego becomes entangled, under the strictures of the Law of Karma, with the unending cycle of birth and death. Frequently, the ego only succeeds in compounding the difficulties in a disciple's attempts towards attaining awareness of God. Unless the ego can stand aside and wait for the Grace of God to descend, it will get nowhere, whereas the bhagtas' devotion to the Lord automatically makes their ego like a recipient of the Divine Grasce and no more, thuys making their success certain.

These five enemies of man — kam (sex), krodh (anger), lobh

(avarice), moh (over-attachment) and ahankar (ego)—are greatly-stimulated by modern society and cannot be subdued until a sincere effort is made to purify our surroundings. The affluent society of the West which seeks sensual pleasures, and the doomed western civilization is having a great influence on the Indian society. We Indians have forgotten our own great heritage of spirituality and culture and have started treating trash as superior to our own inheritance, a situation in which the spiritual initiate has to reorientate himself.

## ENVIRONMENTAL BARRIERS

In the present day society, the individual is exposed to the powerful and perverting influenceds of the mass media; films, radio, television, newspapers, lectures by so-called leaders in the interests of 'progress', all of which are in direct contradiction to the ancient wisdom of India which has always emphasized the superiority of the Spirit over materialism. This meant dedicating oneself to honest labour, not only to keep body and soul together but also generously to assist the weaker sections of society to evolve.

Even in the West, the Kings were originally the protectors of the faith of their subjects. Having lost their position to down-right materialists, who are now the dominant factor, no one appears to be in charge of this function. Even 'Church on Sunday' is out of fashion. Men and women glue themselves on to their transistor sets and listen to the rise and fall of share prices from dusk to dawn. Sex stares at you on every noticeboard you see. Everyone appears to be busy destroying the very framework and foundations of society under the banner of liberalism. Music, which was designed to attune people to their Creator and generate true love amongst humanity, now advertises sex in a most sensuous form. Modern literature no longer contains higher thoughts and ideals, it is full of justification for the so-called basic urges, meaning the passions of human beins. Even heart cases are being advised sex as a cure.

Drinking, dancing and gambling are now the preocc patiof clubs which used to spend a lot of effort in organizing outdoor sports and invigorating treks across mountains and open countryside.

Drugs, which have such a devastating effect on the human brain, are very much in fashion, even in places of learning. From the Government downwards, everyone wants to rob everyone else, since honest labour is no longer fashionable.

There is no respect for the parents or teacher or the elders or the leaders of mankind since none of them owe any responsibility towards those in their care. Teachers are preparing for more lucrative jobs and are more interested in well-paid tuitions; parents, seeking their own pleasure, have no time for the training and education of their children; leaders are busy stabilizing their own position, which they propose to retain in perpetiity.

In modern society, a spiritual plant has to be really very sturdy if it is to grow at all. Inflation, mis-management and corruption at all levels keeps nearly everyone fully engaged in the struggle for material existence. Religious men and women shine like stars in the dark night of an aimless society, making as honest a living as that society allows, giving solace to weaker spirits and setting an example to be followed by all. It is in the thick of battle that a genius makes his mark. Only a 'man' can attempt to overcome such obstacles and be entitled to 'sit with the prophet in his throne, even as he has overcome and sat down with his father in his throne'.

## PSYCHOLOGICAL OBSTACLES

These obstacles are more subtle and obstruct one at the most unexpected times. When the human mind gets used to an idea, however worthless, it finds it extremely hard to give it up. Since reason has rarely played a major part in the faith of an individual, people often cling to anything which their parents or teachers hold in respect. The impressions formed in the early formative period develop a deep groove in the mind of the individual who finds pleasure in the security of that groove. Any innovations at a later stage, during the adolescent period of reasoning, are unwelcome to the mind, which raises all kinds of arguments to justify the existing faith and condemn anything new. People become bigoted and incapable of receiving, much less absorbing, new and, perhaps, more truthful ideas.

If religion is truth, it should be in a position to face the onslaught of any falsehood; it needs no protecting walls. By frank and free discussions and by applying the logical method of analysis, a true religion runs no other risk than that of shedding its dross. By studying comparative religions one will deepen one's faith in one's own religion, if our study shows that other religions can also fulfil one's spiritual needs. The disciple has to free himself fom all bonds before he can qualify for the spiritual ascent.

O Farid, raise up your mind,
By breaking down the barriers.
*Sheikh Baba Farid*

The worst psychological barrier is the human ego. The individual ego gets strengthened by the communal or the so-called 'religious ego' and refuses to acknowledge even the truths in other mens' religions. Many Christians or Moslems or Hindus still believe that the entry to heaven is banned except through their own Gate, but it is blasphemy. Truly spiritual men, following the lead of their prophets, all believe that there are no walls around heaven and that God's children, the human race, can enter from whatever point they like. The various religions are the various paths or disciplines, particularly suited to certain races and countries by following which they can reach the one and only God. Religion is not the name of the Goal or the End itself, it is one of the means to that End. Overzealous disciples often add much formal irrelevancy to their discipline and, in course of time, only this formal element may remain since it is tangible. The spirit, as opposed to the 'letter', which is intangible, disappears. At this stage, the 'form' fights for its identity. So-called religious men fight and incite others to fight, not for any essential truth or essence or spirit but for the external forms. They call these selfish, unjust and unethical wars Crusades or Jihads so that their simple co-religionists enthusiastically die in the hope of

163

an illusory heaven beyond, which they have missed by their own folly in this world.

A story is told about a frog from the ocean who jumped into a well where he met a brother frog who lived there permenently. At this stage, one must appreciate that the ocean frog found the atmosphere in the well a little stuffy.

A conversation ensued somewhat on the following lines:

OCEAN FROG: Brother, how do you pass your time in such confinement?

WELL FROG: It is a big well with a large circumference and I get enough to eat. How big is your well?

OCEAN FROG: Very big.

With a mighty leap the 'well' frog jumped from one end of the well to the other, and said, 'Is your water this big?'

OCEAN FROG: No; much bigger.

WELL FROG: You are lying. Nothing can be bigger than the whole well.

OCEAN FROG: You won't understand until you leave this small well nd see the other creations of God with which you are unfamiliar.

Truth can always stand the test of scrutiny. Nothing is self-sufficient. The ego need not stand in the way of learning from an expert; there is no shame in surrendering to superior wisdom.


## BASIC HURDLES

So far, we have discussed the obstacles to spiritual enlighten-ment which, by diligent and conscienscious effort, can be removed or, at least, weakened. But there are some basic hurdles which cannot be removed in this life, although even here there are some very rare exceptions.

Apparently, some people are, by birth, given to an intensely selfish and materialistic life, which life follows a well-established pattern and nothing, not even the worst of mis-fortunes, will turn those people towards God. They are going through a stage which you may have already passed. There is no point in persuading them to change, for they will do so in God's own time, when their basic urges have been satisfied. This may take several births for an individul. But time is limitless for evolution.

An evil man may put doubts in the mind of the spiritual aspirant about the existence on heavenly justice. One may hear about a well-known criminal, seemingly very prosperous, and then one wonders, 'Is this God's justice?' Over activity, excessive desires can result in sudden heart seizures, schizophrenia and other chronic disorders, which is not real prosperity. In any case, you are only looking aone phase in the long chain of births and deaths of an individual. Any surmise on insufficient data would be wrong. One should consider oneself fortunate in one's present circumstances. God's design is infallible.

> Covet that not which we have bestowed on some sections of the ornaments of this world as a temporary provision so that we may try them thereby. That which the Lord has bestowed on thee is better and more lasting.
>
> *The Holy Koran.* 20: 131.

## THE TRUE ASPIRANT

It will be clear that the aspirant has to have an intense desire to meet his Creator. The journey is long and arduous and needs immense patience. Egotism must be replaced by humility and self-surrender to the chosen guide who should be in touch with God, so that he can lead one there. The aspirant should be prepared to wage a relentless war against the five enemies of sex, anger, avarice, attachment and ego, on the battlefield of worldly life. The aspirant must develop love and compassion for all. Vegetarian food and the company of similarly inclined people will be a great help. Every day of one's life should be used to prepare oneself for the most thrilling adventure of a flight through the astral worlds into the world of the spirit towards God. The very anticipation of this event should produce inebriation, and the consummation of it, perpetual joy. Is it not wonderful to be able to leave the body, embrace the only source of wisdom and perpetual joy and then return to the body and attend to the problem of life with rejuvenated vigour? This is called 'dying daily', in which the soul develops the technique of leaving the body daily—for all practical purposes the body would be taken as dead by anyone if seen at this stage—returning to it at will. Death, the most dreaded thing on earth, no longer holds any fear for the aspirant:

> Death of which the world is afraid,
> Gives me joy.
> Only death puts us in touch
> With infinite joy.
>
> *Kabir*

In some cases, the bodies of such men, while in the stage of 'daily death' have even been cremated by evil-minded successors as in the case of Ram Rai at Dehra Dun.

# 24

## Conclusions

The reader is entitled to draw his own conclusions from this book. My urge and the guru's grace took me to almost all the main spiritual disciplines in vogue in India, although not every one has been mentioned in this book. While I saw some essential truths everywhere, there appeared to be a simultaneous attempt to show each discipline as the only path to God and each of these disciplines was busy constructing walls around itself. Whilst some fencing is necessary to protect the tender saplings from the animals, it should not deprive the plant of fresh air, the sun or the moon, since that will kill it.

Perfece evolution means the all-round development of the individual for which certain elements, or truths may be taken from every discipline which can contribute towards one's development. It should be like consulting specialists in different subjects and incorporating their advice in the composite whole for the benefit of total personality. Some easy and suitable yoga postures and breathing or pranayam exercises, performed regularly, will contribute towards bodily health, which must be done under the guidance of an expert yogi. The aim of utilizing the faculties of a healthy body for achieving awareness of God, and not for physical satisfaction, must never be forgotten.

Developing an aesthetic sense as well as the virtues of non-attachment, selflessness and mind-discipline plays a vital part in the growth of spirituality in man. Some of its best exponents are the Buddhist Lamas of the Mahayana sect. Imbibing their whole philosophy is difficult, a life's work, but the essential points can be more readily grasped and practised. They are also found in Hindu dharma in a somewhat different form.

With a few exceptions, the most evolved Masters have led a family life and faced problems like other common folk. In some cases, their struggle for existence has been very hard, but they have accepted the responsibilities of a family life as well as those of society and have set an example for others to follow. Fulfilling one's responsibilities to one's family first and then elevating oneself to treating the whole of humanity as one's own family can be a very helpful factor in spiritual evolution. Family life is the only field in which one can learn moderation and follow what is called the Middle Path, between asceticism and sensualism. It is, in this battlefield of dharma khand, that the five enemies already sicsussed are to be fought and subdued. It is here that the mind can be disciplined. Forsaking the world and going into the wilderness is a path which suits only a few souls, though the signs are un-mistakable that there is no alternative for that soul. Like Arjuna, however much you dislike the thought, you have to enter the battlefield of kurukshetra and attack and kill your closest kith and kin, in the form of the five enemies. Discipline your mind and surrender it to the loving care of Lord Kirshan, the Charioteer, who has undertaken to instruct you with every turn of the chariot's wheel on this battlefield.

Sacred scriptures and other spiritual literature help to enlarge one's vision, not only the sacred scriptures of the religion one professes but of other religions as well. This broadens the horizon, cleanses and reorientates the mind towards God, consolidates universal truths, steadies one's faith and helps to establish the spiritual goal for each individual. I found the Guru Granth Sahib easily understandable in its ahabharat aso repeated here. The truths expounded by Islam and propagated by the Sufi saints were a constituent part of this sacred book. The Bible appears to be reproduced here in an Indian setting. There is masterly blending of essential truths in all religions in this sacred book. Ultimately, the Guru Granth Sahib attracted my entire attention which I found satisfying to my soul.

Mr Duncan Greenless, in his book 'The Gospel of Guru Granth Sahib', describes the scripture as follows:

> Among the world's scriptures, few, if any, attain so high a literary level or so consistent a height of inspiration.

I found religious company and satwik food most helpful in contributing towards a healthy body and a steady mind, which is capable of prolonged concentration.

When all that has been said earlier has been put into practice, the disciple is ready to receive and nurture the seed, the guru mantra; the Master should be approached to implant the best seed he has, in the most scientific manner. This seed will inevitably grow but it will still depend on the Grace of God, in order to bear the desired fruit.

Each one of us carries within us the power to become a God. The path, though easy and most rewarding, appears difficult and uninteresting owing to the delusion of maya. It is this delusion that has to be destroyed, by first disciplining the mind. A constant struggle has to be waged against the powerful onslaught of the senses which, under the guise of giving pleasure, produce pain and depression, besides eroding the strength of the body. For it is this strength alone, in a concentrated form, which can arouse the latent powers of man. It is a slow process, a very slow one indeed. So the virtues of patience and complete faith have to be developed. The result of this life-long discipline, as proved by spiritual scientists, is so rich that everyone would make a serious attempt at acquiring it, if he could be given some foretaste, something that can only be done by saints who are already living in 'reality' and possess the power to transfer such experiences to beginners.

Think of a man or woman, who is completely fearless having no anxieties of any kind, and all of whose desires are within the power of their father to fulfil.

Think of a 'society' of such fearless and anxiety-free people in which everyone thinks of serving everybody else, with no trace of selfishness; where Love and not hatred or clash of interests is the motivating force; where there are neither exploiter or exploited; where a man is always treated as a man even when he is picked up from a gutter. This would be the heaven that everyone has waited for. It is not Utopia, it already exists. Brave men and women in their hundreds, are disciplining their bodies and minds. But millions more look on undecided. Take the plunge, it is a worthwhile adventure. There is nothing comparable to it in the material world.

Japji, a revelation by Guru Nanak, is, to my mind, the simplified essence of all spiritual truths, enshrined in various scriptures. It is the gita for the devotees who wish to follow the Bhagati marg, the path of devotion. In the very first stanza, God is defined. The praise of the Lord, our Creator and final Goal, is so worded to generate love for Him. The fruits of devotion and obedience to God's will are extolled. God's glory, His splendour, His kindness and Grace, transport one into ecstasy. The path of nam or shabad through Sat Guru is then clearly prescribed. The last few paragraphs describe various stages of spiritual evolution, which only a perfect Master of the calibre of Guru Nanak, could describe. After explaining the Law of Physical Existence on this Earth, which has been called 'dharma sal', the true guide then takes the soul successively up through the

(a) plane of wisdom (gian khand);
(b) plane of effort (or beauty) (saram khand);
(c) plane of Grace or power (karam khand);
(d) plane of Reality (sach khand).

There is a short but beautiful description of each of the planes which have to be traversed by the soul, before it achieves nirvana or moksha, and finally, the great Master describes the disciplines which a disciple has to practise before he or she can contact nam or shabad and Divine Grace. I do not know of anything greater or more fruitful for a disciple, to close this fascinating subject, than with the penultimate stanza of Japji, which enumerates these disciplines.

In this beautiful simile, Nanak Ji prescribes the tools needed in the manufacture of shabad or nam just as they are required by a goldsmith to manufacture an exquisite ornament of beauty.

Chastity the smithy; patience the smith:
Understanding thy anvil, knowledge thy tools:
Fire of austerity; bellows of fear,
The pot of devotion, in it melt thou nectar.
The Word.
In this true mint is coined.
They on whom is Grace, their way is this;
Guru Nanak's love that filleth man with liss.
    *Japji of Guru Nanak   Guru Granh Sahib*

# Glossary of Terms

| | |
|---|---|
| *Allah* | Arabic name for God. |
| *Anand or* | |
| *Pram Anand* | Spiritual bliss or supreme spiritual bliss. |
| *Anhad Nad* | Unstruck sound, heavenly music. |
| *Ashram* | Where renunciates live under a certain discipline. |
| *Atma* | Soul. |
| *Avtar* | Divine incarnation in a human form. |
| *Ayurtedic* | |
| *medicine* | Ancient Hindu system of medicine, using herbs. |
| *Bhagti or* | |
| *Bhakti Yoga* | Devotional and loving remembrance of God. |
| *Bhagawat Gita* | Hindu scripture, comprising Lord Krishna's spiritual exposition to Arjuna, the warrior, on the battlefield of Kurukshetra. |
| *Beej Mantra* | A potencized combination of words given out secretly by a Guru to his disciple, the oral and mental repetition of which energizes the physical centres in the body for spiritual evolution. |
| *Chakra* | Psychic centre in the body. |
| *Darshan* | The Holy appearance or blessing of a saintly person. |
| *Dharam sala* | The abode of Dharma. |
| *Dharma* | Doctrine, the moral laws which help spiritual evolution. |
| *Dhunatmic* | |
| *sounds* | Spiritual sounds or astral music |
| *Diksha* | Initiation. |
| *Durga* | The Goddess of Power, the destroyer of evil. |
| *Faqir* | A Muslim renunciate. . |
| *Guru Granth* | |
| *Sahib* | The revealed scriptures of the Sikh Faith. |
| *Guru* | The spiritual enlightener teacher. |
| *Gurbani* | The revealed hymns uttered by the Guru. |
| *Gyan* | Divine wisdom, gnosis. |
| *Hari or Hare* | The destroyer of Sin; God. |
| *Hanuman* | A great warrior, devotee of Lord Rama symbolised as a Monkey-God. |
| *Hatha yoga* | Physical exercises in order to reach union with God. |

171

| | |
|---|---|
| *Hirdaya* | Heart. |
| *Hukam* | God's will; command. |
| *Ishta* | Ideal chosen for worship. |
| *Jagan Nath* | The Master of Universe; God. |
| *Jap or Japuji or Japji* | Meditational prayer; repetition of God's name or his attributes. |
| *Jihad* | Religious crusade. |
| *Jivan Mukta* | Emancipated from all attachments, with the mind perpetually merged in God while living. |
| *Joti* | The light of pure unalloyed spirit. |
| *Karma* | The law of cause and effect; the combined acts falling under the categories of good and bad, all of which bind the soul to the wheel of birth and death. |
| *Karma Marg* | Path of spiritual evolution through unattached actions in life. |
| *Kirtan (Nam Kirtan)* | Singing the Lord's name. |
| *Kundalini* | Psychic energy, latent in the sacral part of the body, to be developed by Yoga. |
| *Kurukshetra* | The battlefield, where Arjuna, led by Lord Krishna, had to fight his kui (Bhagarad Gita). |
| *Leela* | Divine play. |
| *Lingham or Shiv Ling* | A stone image of spiritual flame (energy), represented as a male organ. |
| *Ma(a)* | Mother. |
| *Nad(a)* | Subtle music heard in a concentrated state of mind. |
| *Nam* | Divine Name, the Word, the Spirit of God. |
| *Nama* | The Neumenon, the holy presence within the body temple. |
| *Onkara* | The ultimate reality. |
| *Pooja* | Worship. |
| *Prana* | Vital current in the cur, the breath. It is distinct from breathing. |
| *Prasad* | Food, blessed by a spiritual person. |
| *Raja Yoga* | The highest yoga. |
| *Rama* | The essence permeating all animate and inanimate objects giving them life; name of God showing all pervasive attribute. |
| *Ridhi* | Miraculous power. |
| *Sabda* | The eternal word. |
| *Sadhu* | One who has mastered a spiritual discipline. |
| *Sahja Yoga* | Spontaneous or patient unhurried union. |
| *Samadhi* | High state of meditation. |

| | |
|---|---|
| *Sainsara* | The world with its cycle of births and deaths. |
| *Sangam* | Union, the place where waters of two or three sacred rivers meet and intermingle. |
| *Sunnyasa* | The final stage of Hindu life, in which a man shuns wordly attachment and reports to ontemplation until his death. Thus it also refers to the condition of all disciples who have forsaken everything in their search for union with God. |
| *Sat* | Reality or Truth. |
| *Sat Guru* | The eternal Guru. |
| *Shabad* | Divine Name. |
| *Shakti* | Goddess of Power; cosmic energy. |
| *Shanti* | Peace of mind. |
| *Shastras* | The six Hindu scriptures. |
| *Shunyata* | Void. |
| *Sidha* | Yogi—the perfect one. |
| *Sidhi* | Occult powers acquired by yogis after several austerities. These powers are also acquired through intense devotion and love of God. |
| *Sikh* | Disciple; a member of a distinct faith believing in Guru Granth Sahib, the Sikh scripture. |
| *Shiva* | The destroyer aspect in the Hindu Trinity. Also used as a name of God. |
| *Sukhmani* | Gem of Peace; a composition of Guru Arjun, the recitation of which cleanses the mind and brings peace. |
| *Tantra* | A system of Penances practiced on cremation grounds. |
| *Tapasya* | Yoga austerities. |
| *Upanishads* | Sacred scriptures of the Hindus. |
| *Vairag* | Divine indifference to the world of attachment. |
| *Vishnu* | The sustainer aspect of the Hindu Trinity. |
| *Yoga* | Union; spiritual merger with God. |
| *Yogi* | One merged in God. The common meaning is one who practises physical and breathing exercises to achieve union with ultimate reality. |
| *Yuga* | One of the four ages of the world, i.e. Satyuga—the age of truth or perfection. Trefta—when only three quarters of truth remain. Dwapar—when two quarters or half of truth remains. Kaliyuga—the machine age of falsehood in which we live today. |
| *Vedas* | The revealed scriptures of Hindus; four in number. |
| *Wajad* | State of elevation. |

# Bibliography

The Holy Bible (Old and New Testament) — The Gideons International.

The Greatest is Love — BIBLES for the world, New Delhi. India.

The Holy Quran
The Sufi Message of Hasrat Inayat Khan 12 volumes). — Serrire l.v., 5A, Lydeweg, Wassenaar, Holland.

The Guru Granth Sahib (English Version) by Dr Gopal Singh. — Dur Das Kapoor & Sons Pvt. Ltd. — Delhi.

The Gospel of the Guru Granth Sahib by Duncan Greenlees — The Theosophical Publishing House, Adyar, Madras, India.

The Path of the Masters by Julian Johnson. — Sawan Service League, Beas, India.

The Bhagavad Gita translated by Dr Radha Krishnan — George Allen & Unwin Ltd., Ruskin House, Muslim Street, London WC1.

The Hindu view of life by Dr Radha Krishnan. — George Allen & Unwin Ltd. Ruskin House, Musium Street, London WC1.

The wisdom of the Hindus by Brian Brown. — Garden City Publicity Co. Inc Garden City, New York.

Dev Atma Shakti by Vishnu Tirtha. — Shankarlalji Bhatnagar, Dabra-Gwalior (MP) India.

Our Master, Shri Sita Ram Das Onkarnath by Sadananda Chakrabarti. — Mahamilan Math — PWD Road, Calcutta — 35

Mystics and Society by Sisir Kumar Ghose. — Asia Publishing House, New Delhi.

The Autobiography of a Yogi by Paramhansa Yogananda. — Yogoda Satsang Society of India, Dakshineswar P. O. Ariadaha, 24, Parganas, West Bengal, India.

The Holy Science by Yukteswar Giri
Bhaktiyoga by Swami Vivekananda — ,, ,, ,, ,, ,, ,, Advarita Ashrama, 4, Wilhington Lane, Calcutta — 13.

The Adhi Grauth — transl. by Dr E. Trump. — Munshiram Mansharlal, New Delhi.

174

transl. by Dr E. Trump.

Ten Upanishads by Swami Sivananda.

Fourteen lessons on Rajdyoga by Swami Sivananda.

Spiritual experiences by Swami Sivananda.

What becomes of the Soul after death by Swami Sivananda.

The Science of Yoga — 7 Vols

The Yoga System of Health by Vithal Das

Sai Baba, Man of Miracles by Howard Murphet.

Founding the Life Divine Sri Aurobindo by Morwenna Donnelly.

Swami Muktananda Param-Khansa by Amma

Yoga by Earnest Wood.

Budhist Texts — Edited by Edward Conze.

My land and my people by the Dalai Lama.

Selections from the sacred writings of the Sikhs.

Inayat Khan — a biography by L. de Jang-Keesing.

Sai Baba of Shindi by John Osborne.

Sufi saints and shrines by John A. Subhan

Words of Shri Quandamay Na.

The Crown of life by Sant Kirpal Swigh

Play of Consciousness by Swami Muktananda.

Munshiram Mansharlal, New Delhi.

The Divine Life Society — Po Shivananda Nagar Harishikish — UP India.

,,    ,,    ,,    ,,    ,,    ,,    ,,

,,    ,,    ,,    ,,    ,,    ,,    ,,

,,    ,,    ,,    ,,    ,,    ,,    ,,
,,    ,,    ,,    ,,    ,,    ,,    ,,

Faber & Faber Ltd., 24 Russell Square, London.

The Macmillan Company of India Ltd. Madras.

Jaico Public House 125, Mahatma Gandi Road, Bombay — 1.

Vora & Co., Publication Pvt. Ltd. 3, Round Building, Bombay — 2.

Penguin Books Ltd, Harmondsworth, Middlesex, England.

Bruno Cassiver (Publications) Ltd, 31 Portland Road, Oxford.

Mcgraw-Hill Book Co. Inc, New York.

George Allen & Unwin Ltd, Museum Street, London.

East-West Publications Fonts b.v. Postbox 7617, The Hague, Holland.

Longmans Orient, Madras, India.

Samuel Weiser, 11g Broadway, New York.

Shree Shree Quandamayec Saugha, Varanasi.

Ruhani Satsaug, Sawan Ashram, New Delhi — 7.

Shri Suruder Siddha Yogi Ashram, California.

175